P9-EEU-657

COMPREHENSIVE RESEARCH
AND STUDY GUIDE

John
Donne

EDITED AND WITH AN INTRODUCTION
BY HAROLD BLOOM

BLOOM'S MAJOR DRAMATISTS

Anton Chekhov
Henrik Ibsen
Arthur Miller
Eugene O'Neill
Shakespeare's Comedies
Shakespeare's Histories
Shakespeare's Romances
Shakespeare's Tragedies
George Bernard Shaw
Tennessee Williams

BLOOM'S MAJOR NOVELISTS

Jane Austen
The Brontës
Willa Cather
Charles Dickens
William Faulkner
F. Scott Fitzgerald
Nathaniel Hawthorne
Ernest Hemingway
Toni Morrison
John Steinbeck
Mark Twain
Alice Walker

BLOOM'S MAJOR SHORT STORY WRITERS

William Faulkner
F. Scott Fitzgerald
Ernest Hemingway
O. Henry
James Joyce
Herman Melville
Flannery O'Connor
Edgar Allan Poe
J. D. Salinger
John Steinbeck
Mark Twain
Eudora Welty

BLOOM'S MAJOR WORLD POETS

Geoffrey Chaucer
Emily Dickinson
John Donne
T. S. Eliot
Robert Frost
Langston Hughes
John Milton
Edgar Allan Poe
Shakespeare's Poems & Sonnets
Alfred, Lord Tennyson
Walt Whitman
William Wordsworth

BLOOM'S NOTES

The Adventures of Huckleberry Finn
Aeneid
The Age of Innocence
Animal Farm
The Autobiography of Malcolm X
The Awakening
Beloved
Beowulf
Billy Budd, Benito Cereno, & Bartleby the Scrivener
Brave New World
The Catcher in the Rye
Crime and Punishment
The Crucible

Death of a Salesman
A Farewell to Arms
Frankenstein
The Grapes of Wrath
Great Expectations
The Great Gatsby
Gulliver's Travels
Hamlet
Heart of Darkness & The Secret Sharer
Henry IV, Part One
I Know Why the Caged Bird Sings
Iliad
Inferno
Invisible Man
Jane Eyre
Julius Caesar

King Lear
Lord of the Flies
Macbeth
A Midsummer Night's Dream
Moby-Dick
Native Son
Nineteen Eighty-Four
Odyssey
Oedipus Plays
Of Mice and Men
The Old Man and the Sea
Othello
Paradise Lost
A Portrait of the Artist as a Young Man
The Portrait of a Lady

Pride and Prejudice
The Red Badge of Courage
Romeo and Juliet
The Scarlet Letter
Silas Marner
The Sound and the Fury
The Sun Also Rises
A Tale of Two Cities
Tess of the D'Urbervilles
Their Eyes Were Watching God
To Kill a Mockingbird
Uncle Tom's Cabin
Wuthering Heights

COMPREHENSIVE RESEARCH
AND STUDY GUIDE

John
Donne

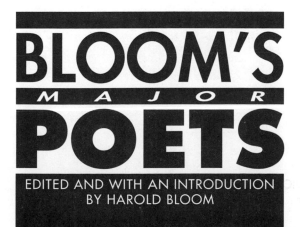

BLOOM'S *MAJOR*
POETS

EDITED AND WITH AN INTRODUCTION
BY HAROLD BLOOM

© 1999 by Chelsea House Publishers, a subsidiary of Haights Cross Communications.

Introduction © 1999 by Harold Bloom

All rights reserved. No part of this publication may be reproduced or transmitted in any form or by any means without the written permission of the publisher.

Printed and bound in the United States of America.

3 5 7 9 8 6 4

Library of Congress Cataloging-in-Publication Data

John Donne : comprehensive research and study guide / edited and with an introduction by Harold Bloom.
cm. – (Bloom's major poets)
ISBN 0-7910-5116-1 (hc)
1. Donne, John, 1572-1631—Criticism and interpretation—handbooks, manuals, etc.   2. Donne, John,
1572-1631—Examinations—Study guides.   I. Bloom, Harold.
II. Series.
PR2248.J59   1999
821'.3—dc21
98-53871
CIP

Chelsea House Publishers
1974 Sproul Road, Suite 400
Broomall, PA 19008-0914

Contributing Editor: Janyce Marson

ACC Library Services
Austin, Texas

Contents

User's Guide

This volume is designed to present biographical, critical, and bibliographical information on the author's best-known or most important poems. Following Harold Bloom's editor's note and introduction is a detailed biography of the author, discussing major life events and important literary accomplishments. A thematic and structural analysis of each poem follows, tracing significant themes, patterns, and motifs in the work.

A selection of critical extracts, derived from previously published material from leading critics, analyzes aspects of each poem. The extracts consist of statements from the author, if available, early reviews of the work, and later evaluations up to the present. A bibliography of the author's writings (including a complete list of all books written, cowritten, edited, and translated), a list of additional books and articles on the author and the work, and an index of themes and ideas in the author's writings conclude the volume.

～

Harold Bloom is Sterling Professor of the Humanities at Yale University and Henry W. and Albert A. Berg Professor of English at the New York University Graduate School. He is the author of over 20 books and the editor of more than 30 anthologies of literary criticism.

Professor Bloom's works include *Shelley's Mythmaking* (1959), *The Visionary Company* (1961), *Blake's Apocalypse* (1963), *Yeats* (1970), *A Map of Misreading* (1975), *Kabbalah and Criticism* (1975), and *Agon: Toward a Theory of Revisionism* (1982). *The Anxiety of Influence* (1973) sets forth Professor Bloom's provocative theory of the literary relationships between the great writers and their predecessors. His most recent books include *The American Religion* (1992), *The Western Canon* (1994), *Omens of Millennium: The Gnosis of Angels, Dreams, and Resurrection* (1996), and *Shakespeare: The Invention of the Human* (1998).

Professor Bloom earned his Ph.D. from Yale University in 1955 and has served on the Yale faculty since then. He is a 1985 MacArthur Foundation Award recipient and served as the Charles Eliot Norton Professor of Poetry at Harvard University in 1987–88. He is currently the editor of other Chelsea House series in literary criticism, including BLOOM'S NOTES, BLOOM'S MAJOR SHORT STORY WRITERS, MAJOR LITERARY CHARACTERS, MODERN CRITICAL VIEWS, MODERN CRITICAL INTERPRETATIONS, and WOMEN WRITERS OF ENGLISH AND THEIR WORKS.

Editor's Note

My Introduction contrasts the Platonic passion of "The Ecstasie" with the Christian fervor of "A Hymn to God the Father." It is the mingling of those strains that is caught so subtly and learnedly by the copious extracts that make up the most vital portion of this volume. The titans of Donne-criticism are assembled here, and I commend them all to the reader.

Introduction

HAROLD BLOOM

Donne's mode has been so influential, both in the Seventeenth and the Twentieth century, that we are likely to forget that his ambivalent tonalities were radically idiosyncratic. At once pious and skeptical, Donne's stance, by paradox, may have been best appreciated in the Nineteenth Century. His libertine poetry, I suspect, will be most widely diffused in the Twenty-First Century, since it gives form to impulses otherwise inchoate. Donne's wit—allusive, harsh, sardonic, able to digest astonishing diversities—is an apt instrument for a post-erotic age, like the one we soon will enter.

I will confine myself here to two poems, "The Ecstasie" and "A Hymn to God the Father." "The Ecstasie"'s title refers to the lovers' "standing outside" one another's bodies, in a charmed interval between renewed intercourse. Fused (momentarily) into one Platonic soul, the lovers must return to merger lest their composite soul be rendered powerless: "Else a great prince in prison lies." The truths of the revealed religion of love depend upon the sexual body as Bible: "But yet the body is his book."

If we listen closely to this adroit "dialogue of one," then we will cease to distinguish between the "ecstasy" that is a standing back and the other ectasy "when we are to bodies gone." If this is a seduction poem, it is a permanent one, as likely to be effective centuries hence as it may have been four centuries ago.

The holy John Donne is fused with the libertine wit, never more perhaps than in "A Hymn to God the Father." Punning sublimely upon his own name, the Dean of St. Paul's intricately voyages forth to meet God as welcoming father, in a hymn of faith that deserves contrast to the skeptical Hamlet's meditations upon death as the undiscovered country from whose bourn no traveler returns. Donne, in the Christian ecstasy of belief, awaits Resurrection:

> I have a sin of fear, that when I have spun
> My last thread, I shall perish in the shore;
> But swear by thy self, that at my death thy son
> Shall shine as he shines now, and heretofore;
> And, having done that, thou hast done,
> I fear no more.

Biography of
John Donne

(1572–1631)

John Donne was born in 1572 into an old Roman Catholic family, at a time when Catholics were being persecuted in England and even harassed by the authorities. It was an era when those Catholics who chose to openly practice their religion were at times barred from pursuing successful careers. In John Carey's biography on Donne, entitled *John Donne: His Life, Mind and Art,* Carey describes the penalty for choosing to publicly practice Catholicism as both limiting and sometimes dangerous. Legislation made Catholics' lives almost impossible, for it denied them legal redress against state-sanctioned persecution. "You could not, if you remained faithful to your religion, hope to play any part in public life, and you were debarred from taking a university degree by the requirement that graduates should subscribe to the Thirty-nine Articles," Carey wrote.

This world into which Donne was born was all the more terrifying because of his family's Catholic connections; he was even made to witness public executions. Carey suggests that Donne witnessed these while in the care of his Catholic tutors, who hoped to cultivate a strong sense of martyrdom in the young boy. Donne's family history fully supports the importance of sacrifice for belief. His grandfather, John Heywood, was forced to flee rather than accept the state religion, Anglicanism, and he saw his neighbors arrested and put to death. Donne eventually saw compromise as the only way out of this terrible predicament, and he quietly abandoned Catholicism in the 1590s.

Though he studied at Oxford and Cambridge universities, and attended Lincoln's Inn (where lawyers in those days received their training), he did not take any academic degrees and never practiced law. He lacked a talent for a business, and he inherited no family fortune. As a result, for a while Donne had to make his way in the world relying on his wit, charm, and intelligence. He read enormously in religion, medicine, law, and the classics, and he wrote to display the magnitude of that learning. He also was able to travel widely throughout the Continent and placed himself in court employment.

In 1598 Donne was appointed secretary to Thomas Egerton, one of the highest officials in Queen Elizabeth's court. However, in 1601 Donne undermined those political achievements by secretly marrying Anne More, Lady Egerton's seventeen-year-old niece. Although the marriage turned out to be a happy one, with Donne maintaining absolute fidelity to his wife, he paid a heavy price for his actions. He was dismissed from his post and then imprisoned; following that imprisonment, Donne's opportunities for earning a living were severely curtailed. At a time when his wife was giving birth almost once a year, Donne was in a wretched state, constantly worrying how to support his growing family.

In fact, during this time of personal downfall, Donne wrote an unpublished treatise, entitled *Biathanatos*, on the lawfulness of suicide. This morbid interest should be understood within the context of the times in which Donne lived, the scenes and stories of martyrdom from his earliest days, and his interest in a theory of universal flux, which viewed life as a perpetual dying.

Despite Donne's outright refusal to take Anglican orders in 1607, King James believed that Donne would one day become a great Anglican preacher. Accordingly, the king declared that Donne's only avenue for success and financial security would be through the Church. Donne wrote an anti-Catholic polemic in 1610, which contained ludicrous examples of miraculous saints' lives; in 1611, he also wrote a satire against the Jesuits entitled *Ignatius His Conclave*. He was obviously in the process of overcoming his scruples against ordination, and he entered the Anglican ministry in 1615.

This act could conceivably be used as evidence for his ambition, rather than his spirituality. Indeed, throughout his life Donne had a constant desire for work and worldly success. However, he saw these as almost religious duties. Preaching was thus a natural occupation for someone of Donne's intellectual abilities and energy. It afforded him an opportunity to write and speak publicly on spiritual and intellectual matters, while at the same time providing him a vehicle for his dramatic talents. Donne's boldness, wit, and learning soon made him into a great preacher, and in 1621 he was made Dean of St. Paul's.

Three years later a book of his private prayers and devotions were published. One hundred and sixty of his sermons also survive. Throughout his life he continued to write sacred poetry, right up until his death.

He was obsessed with the idea of death, and even went as far as composing his own terrifying funeral sermon, "Death's Duel," shortly before he died. He also commissioned a self-portrait in which he wore a funeral shroud. The circumstances of this self-portrait are every bit as dramatic and startling as his written work. Having purchased a large wooden urn, Donne dressed himself in a shroud, with knots tied at head and foot, and then balanced himself atop the urn, where he remained while his portrait was being drawn. All of these deathbed theatrics gave testimony to his need for control. After delivering "Death's Duel," his final sermon, he died on March 31, 1631.

While John Donne and his followers, George Herbert, Richard Crashaw, Henry Vaughn, and others, have been known to literary history as the "metaphysical" school, this was certainly not a name they applied to themselves. Instead, the term "metaphysical" was conferred on them by Samuel Johnson, in his essay on the poet Abraham Cowley in *Lives of the Poets*, written in 1779.

Johnson stated that this group of poets "were men of learning, and to show their learning was their whole endeavor." He compounded this unflattering portrait by suggesting that the "metaphysical" school had not earned the privilege of calling themselves poets "for they cannot be said to have imitated anything: they neither copied nature nor life, neither painted the forms of matter nor represented the operations of the intellect." Samuel Johnson, however, was writing almost a century and a half later as a leading figure of the neoclassical age. Neoclassicism sought to reformulate the literary values of ancient Greece and Rome, and a part of the classical agenda was to construct a more direct and faithful representation of nature, most especially human nature.

Donne, on the other hand, wrote in a much different literary climate. He was influenced by the experimentation of other contemporary Continental poets, who were striking out against a tradition of highly stylized poetic clichés, such as bleeding hearts, cheeks like roses, and Cupids shooting arrows. These had been employed by the poetry of courtly love, a tradition that was nourished by literary texts and consisted of poetry written to and about the aristocracy. This poetry depicted the relationship between a knight and his lady, describing the knight's protestations of unworthiness and his endless pursuit of danger and adventure to prove his faithful and devoted service to his lady.

Donne was also writing against the backdrop of a religious and literary tradition, begun in the early Middle Ages, that held that the body and soul were distinct. This tradition believed that the present life was one of self-denial. The everlasting peace of the soul in the next world would compensate for this renunciation of passion and sexuality. In other words, the suffering and tribulations of this world would all be rewarded by the soul's future happiness in the world to come. Conversely, frightening images of damnation waited for those who sinned.

Finally, the literature produced during the long span of the Middle Ages was driven by a strategy for reading and composition that began with the early monks' method of explicating the Bible. It consisted in discovering hidden messages beyond the actual printed word. This method, known as allegorical interpretation, began as a strategy of interpretation and, shortly thereafter, became the prescribed way to compose imaginative literature. As far back as Aelfric in the eighth century, the church was anxious that those who were only partially literate, and thus not trained to read an allegory, were in danger of going far astray.

After the Middle Ages, literature tried to repair the divorce between body and soul. This rhetorical division between body and soul had been so pervasive that after the Renaissance literature became deeply engaged with the effort to repair this rift. Donne's poetry, as well as that of the other metaphysical poets, sought to establish a way of inseparably uniting the body and soul in this world; it strenuously affirmed human sexuality as a way to achieve spirituality. Indeed, Donne dared to use erotic imagery and at times even bawdy or slang terminology, in complete opposition to what had been considered appropriate and decorous previously. Thus, in his bold and often incongruous imagery, Donne broke away from the past and offered new and brilliant ways to perceive reality and the spiritual nature of our secular existence. ❀

General Introduction to
Songs and Sonnets

In 1633, two years after John Donne's death, a a collection of his poems entitled *Songs and Sonnets* was published. In its most general sense, *Songs and Sonnets* is a collection that deals with amorous themes. Before we can take our analysis of the poems beyond this point, however, we need to understand the rich literary tradition that served as these poem's background. Only then can we fully comprehend and appreciate Donne's artistic achievement.

That artistic achievement also reveals his political agenda. In addition, it gives us insight into his intellectual and emotional response to the turbulent times in which he lived. Therefore, a brief overview of the literary tradition which Donne inherited, and the rhetorical devices he employed, is essential before analyzing the theme and structure of the individual poems.

The concept of conceit is vital in Donne's poetry. A conceit is a complex and arresting metaphor, an implied comparison, which causes us to work hard to retrieve the multi-faceted meanings of individual words and images. The word is derived from the Italian word *concetto*, meaning concept, and in Donne's poetry (and in the poetry of those who were influenced by him), a conceit is a rhetorical operation that is specifically intellectual rather than sensuous. The device creates impossible relations. Consequently, the technique makes strenuous demands upon readers, asking us to combine objects and ideas in new and unconventional ways. The result allows us to perceive the world in a new way. This shifting emphasis on the intellectual content of the poem as opposed to the sensuous refocuses prior literary tradition, specifically, the literary traditions that pertain to the sonnet.

A sonnet is a fourteen-line poem of varying rhyme schemes. It flourished during the 14th century in Italy in the poetry of Francesca Petrarca (1304–1374). Structurally, the Italian sonnet (the most prevalent type) is divided into two parts: stanza of eight lines (an octave) that contains a complete thought, followed by an implicit pause to indicate a turn of thought, and another six lines (a sestet) that forms the conclusion, which is characteristically both unpredictable and intense. This particular form of the sonnet is Petrarchan, and belongs to the literary tradition of courtly love that dates back to 12th-century Europe, most especially in France.

The courtly love tradition codified the rules by which the courtly lover paid homage to his idealized noble passion for his lady. This tradition was essentially medieval and chivalric, based on the duty of a knight to pledge his loyalty to both his lord and his lady; since medieval knights belonged to the aristocratic class of landowners, the convention has important social and political implications as well.

Thus, the courtly love tradition included worship of a lady who was in an exalted position above the lover, as well as the idea that the lover gains nobility through his service to her. The knight expends a great deal of effort lamenting his feelings of unworthiness, and his longing for the woman is driven by a desire to be united with her in both body and soul. The goal of this union is not the satisfaction of passionate desire but, rather, the achievement of moral perfection. However, within this tradition of noble purpose, the poems sometimes deal with adulterous relationships; almost always they are about unrequited love. In a word, the amorous situation is an impossible one.

John Donne broke the rules of all these courtly traditions. For Donne, as we will see, the word *sonnet* defines, in general terms, simply a love lyric; it does not adhere to any formal structure.

In each of the poems discussed in this book, we will examine the "metaphysical" conceit, inaugurated by John Donne, and the ways in which it created new and unique ways of looking at the world. At the same time, Donne sought to subvert or resist the literary conventions on which the the his work was based. In each instance, the title of the poem serves as the entrée into each poem's particular conceit. ❀

Thematic Analysis of "The Good Morrow"

Many modern scholars consider "The Good Morrow" to be the first poem of *Songs and Sonnets*. Like the other poems in this volume, is investigates the nature of true love, but it does so in a far more serious mode than many of the other poems in this collection. The title of the poem suggests that it is a salutation, a greeting to the dawn of a new day.

The poem begins as a highly dramatic poem in which the speaker captures our immediate attention with the exclamation "I wonder, by my troth, what thou and I / Did, till we loved? Were we not weaned till then." Thus, we find out immediately that the specific dawning to which this poem refers is the awakening of sexual awareness, and further, the speaker's reference to sexuality is in earnest, "by my troth"; in other words, he is interested in finding and living up to the requirements of true love rather than mere sexual dalliance. This is a physical love, however, rather than purely spiritual, as the words "sucked" and "snorted" underline. This faithful and sexual love is something far more satisfying than a "fanciful" literary convention, as depicted in the courtly love tradition.

The first stanza also tells us that the lovers are not innocents but rather old hands at love. The love affair here has strong implications of spiritual revelation. There is also, in the phrase "the seven sleepers' den," a reference to a Christian and Mohammedan legend of the seven youths of Ephesus who hid in a cave for 187 years so as to avoid pagan persecution during the dawn of Christianity. This literary reference underscores the implication of dawning spirituality.

In the second stanza, this nascent spirituality is clearly indicated. "And now good morrow to our waking souls." That spirituality is a liberating one, for they no longer "watch not one another out of fear," but instead see with great clarity: "For love all love of other sights controls, / And makes one little room an everywhere." Indeed, so liberating is this new sense of the spiritual that it expands the horizons of their vision and transforms a small space into an entire world. Furthermore, faith in their convictions renders them courageous, unlike the example in the first stanza of the "seven sleepers" who had no choice but to hide from pagan persecution. As the fullest expression of their faith, the lovers are willing to allow others to pursue adventures: "Let sea-discoverers to new worlds have gone." In possessing one another, each has gained world enough. "Let us possess one world, each hath one, and is one." Thus, implicit within this second stanza is the perspective that two worlds are being juxtaposed, the sensual world of restless "map readers" versus the feeling of contentment and emotional balance of the spiritual world in which the lovers now live as a result of their awakening. This juxtaposition of the sensual with the spiritual suggests that those who live solely in the sensual world, busying themselves in mundane matters, are lost to the world of true love.

In the next and final stanza, Donne expands the conceit of world exploration to present us with a further distinction between the spirituality of the lovers and the "map reader" and "sea-discoverers." These pursue grandiose yet vague goals, such as the uncharted territory of new lands, while the lovers develop a very minute and precise vision, the sort of sight that comes with true love. Here, the eyes, traditionally considered the gateway to the soul, become attuned to truth. "My face in thine eye, thine in mine appears, / And true plain hearts do in the faces rest." Peace and contentment now prevail, in sharp contrast not only to the fickleness of the world, but also to the high energy of the first stanza when the lovers first entered the spiritual realm. The lovers' thoughts are now turned to abstract and philosophical questions, and ultimately the poem deals with absolute faith and belief in the immortality of the soul. "Whatever dies was not mixed equally; If our two loves be one, or thou and I / Love so alike that none to slacken, none can die." ❀

Thematic Analysis of "The Sunne Rising"

"The Sunne Rising," another poem contained within the volume *Songs and Sonnets*, begins with the poet taking an oppositional stance toward nature—specifically the dawning of a new day—because it has intruded on the poet and his lover. Donne addresses the sun with extreme brusqueness, calling it a "busy old fool" who nettles in romantic relationships. He chastises it for its relentless pursuit of the poet. "Why dost thou thus / Through windows and through curtains call on us? / Must to thy motions lovers' seasons run?" Indeed we are made to feel that the sun is an oppressive "being" the poet wishes to banish—or at least direct it to others who have need of its intrusive reminder that there is work to be done.

Obviously, the sun is the conceit employed in this poem. The sun belongs to the everyday world of mundane concerns and preoccupation with time, a world that all true lovers seek to renounce. Donne would be happy to redirect the sun's attentions to "late schoolboys" and "sour prentices" (who were legally bound to perform work while learning a trade). Contained within the conceit of the sun in pursuit is yet another allusion to the prototypical quest motif that was fundamental to medieval romance; as always, Donne, as a poet, takes care to contradict the legitimacy of romantic thought. Thus, when he refers to the sun as a "[s]aucy pedantic wretch," the economy of the conceit is again revealed, underscoring the poet's artistic agenda: to do away with books, specifically, the idealized and highly decorative medieval tales of knights in pursuit of love and adventure, in favor of far more realistic descriptions of love. Indeed, in the last line of the first stanza, the phrase "rags of time" makes us think of the remnants of medieval lore, the torn fragments of a tightly woven formulaic method of storytelling.

Yet for all of his protestation, we do not sense that the poet is able to banish this "busy old fool." Instead, he wrestles with its tyrannical presence, exerting enormous energy in the process. Likewise, the poet's rebellion against a centuries-old literary tradition cannot be done casually but instead requires an equally relentless struggle.

The second stanza continues the conversation with the sun, but here the sun has assumed a religious power: "Thy beams, so reverend and strong." Nonetheless, the poet adopts an irreverent posture, expressing his wish to dispose of this divine power in a cavalier fashion, boasting that "I could eclipse and cloud them with a wink."

This is yet a further extension of the lover's resistance to nature's intrusions. The lover will, he claims, almost instantaneously ("in a wink") deprive the sun of its radiance and life-giving powers, by causing some object to obscure its light. This image expresses the lovers' extreme defiance: they would rather revel amorously in an eternal nighttime than endure the sun's continual interruption.

The poet also wishes to subvert those literary forebears who threaten to "eclipse" and overshadow his own originality. Interestingly, the word *eclipse*, in its Greek origin, meant to forsake an accustomed place or to fail to appear. This further supports the idea that the lover would like to exile the sun—and also erase the literary tradition that influenced his artistic sensibilities.

Nonetheless, for all of his proud boasting, the poet/lover doubts the success of his mission. He recognizes that a victory over the sun would at the same time mean a defeat, because an eclipse of the sun would banish the light that is necessary to gaze upon his lover. "But that I would not lose her sight so long." Likewise, a denial of poetic influence will similarly eclipse his own creative achievement, for it would prevent him from comparing his poetry with what has gone before; that comparison is the very thing that gives form and substance to his work.

Implicit in the sun's banishment is the loss of time, because light is also a metaphor for perspective and the ability to compare ourselves to what has gone before. "Ask for those kings whom thou saw'st yesterday, / And thou shalt hear, All here in one bed lay." History itself is in danger of being erased. The second stanza thus ends in a deadlock.

Thematic Analysis of
"Song"

Some have thought that this poem within the *Songs and Sonnets* evidences Donne's contempt for women. However, although Donne held conservative views on women, believing that a wife should be chaste, sober, and quiet, and that intellectual accomplishments were not necessary, the contempt he implies in this poem is probably best seen as "literary"; in other words, his agenda in this poem is to completely overturn the Petrarchan tradition of love poetry, the adoration for the lady.

From a literary standpoint, the poem is satirical, which is to say that it criticizes the courtly love tradition. Satire, in a broader sense, can be a mode of writing that enables the poet/author to berate the shortcomings and values of the times in which he lives. Implicit within the satiric mode is the idea that the poet may possibly have a playful attitude toward his work.

However, this poem can also be read as a revelation of the speaker's loss of confidence in his beloved. He doubts her faithfulness and experiences a general disillusionment with women. If we opt for a psychological interpretation rather than a "literary" one, then the courtly love tradition is a vehicle through which Donne can articulate his frustration.

In either interpretation, the love relationship is an impossible one. Indeed, as the first line of this poem indicates ("go and catch a falling star"), true love is presented as an impossible task. The speaker's frustration is expressed by increasingly absurd instructions, as in the famous line: "Get with child a mandrake root."

This impossible demand is a perfect illustration of the economy of multiple meanings inherent in the conceit. To begin with, a mandrake root is a vegetable; obviously, it is not able to conceive a human being. The shape of the mandrake root, however, is forked like the lower part of the human anatomy, and thus, by association, it is used here as a substitute for human genitalia. Such a union, were it possible, would be barren.

This underlines that no vital and productive relationship can exist between the speaker and his "other"; the speaker is so distraught that he suggests that he sees no hope for the future. This is unlike the art of complaint for the absent love object in the courtly love tradition, where hope for the future was indefinitely sustained by the courtly lover of the Petrarchan tradition.

To further underscore this loss of hope, the speaker's requests take on a cosmic dimension of impossibility—for instance, the directive to recapture that which cannot be grasped, time itself: "Tell me where all past years are." This is soon followed by another request: "Teach me to hear mermaids singing." All the requests are doomed to failure because of the treacherous and seductive nature of women.

This particular image is culled from *The Odyssey*. The singing mermaids alludes to the sirens, mythological beings, part woman and part bird, who lured sailors to their death with their beautiful and intoxicating voices. Only the hero Odysseus was able to stave off their temptation. The image of the sirens is an image of sterility, a conflation of human and animal, which reinforces the impossibility of a loving and fertile relationship between the speaker and his lady. The poem depicts an imaginary world devoid of any hope for future fulfillment.

One of the other rhetorical terms that applies to the metaphysical mode of writing is *catachresis,* a Greek word that means misuse. In literary terms, it can be defined as a very unusual definition or misapplication of a word, producing a strained comparison or effect. Donne uses this technique in "Song" to suggest that love itself is only a literary convention, invented by the poets; it has nothing to do with the reality of our mortal experiences.

The second stanza continues with an even more direct command; the poet asks that we test his theory by embarking on a journey to find fulfillment in love, just as the knights and lovers of the medieval romance did. "If thou beest born to strange sights, / . . . Ride ten thousand days and nights, / Till age snow white hairs on thee." The fulfillment of this command is portrayed as being so exhausting as to persuade us not to even make the attempt. Furthermore, as part of Donne's agenda to dissuade us from even entertaining the thought of such vain pursuits, the poet predicts the outcome of that romantic quest, a future which is closed off from any possibility of fulfillment. Unlike the knights of legend who rode off in quest of strange and wondrous deeds in order to prove themselves worthy to their lady, the lover's mission is doomed to failure. "Thou, when thou return'st, wilt tell me . . . No where / Lives a woman true, and fair."

That utter disillusionment is then carried into the next and final stanza of the poem. Here the poet challenges us to prove him wrong by finding a lady who is both fair and true. "If thou find'st one, let me know, / Such a pilgrimage were sweet; / Yet do not, I would not go." The use of the word "pilgrimage" lends a spiritual tone to the lovers' union, reminding us of the medieval journey that pilgrims took to the Holy Land or to a site of religious significance. The pilgrimage was, in reality, difficult and physically demanding, but it also served as an opportunity for spiritual growth along the way to one's ultimate destination. The pilgrimage concept played an important part in the courtly love tradition, with the culmination of that journey ending in spiritual and physical union with the woman. However, even if we claim to have found that ideal woman, Donne will have none of it, because he will not allow himself to entertain the thought that love is possible with one who is both true and fair. "Though she were true when you met her . . . Yet she / Will be/ False, ere I come, to two or three."

Thus, although true love may be possible for some, the mental state of the poet of this poem is so extreme that he places himself outside the realm of future happiness and fulfillment. This was his position at the outset of the poem, and it remains unchanged at the end.

The poem contains strenuous images, demanding an enormous expenditure of energy if the reader is to ferret out their imaginative potential. Despite the poem's cynical tone, the result suggests that the mythic and the supernatural are much closer to reality than we might have thought previously. ❀

Critical Views on
"The Good Morrow,"
"The Sun Rising," and "Song"

RODNEY EDGECOMB ON "THE SUNNE RISING"
AND *KING LEAR*

[Rodney Edgecomb is the author of '*Sweetnesse readie penn'd: Imagery, Syntax and Metrics in the Poetry of George Herbert* (1980). In the excerpt below from his article "An Enquiry into the Syntax of Donne's 'The Good-morrow' and "The Sunne Rising," Edgecomb discusses "The Sunne Rising" as a satire, comparing it to an example from *King Lear* in which Kent insults Oswald, and also indicates some of the important tensions within the sun conceit.]

Whereas the silent auditor of "The Good-morrow" is the beloved herself, "The Sunne Rising", an altogether more roystering poem, directs its vocatives outwards, and with the same mock-irritability that characterizes the opening lines of "The Canonization". The title once again bears analysis, for it reveals the poem to be a satiric version of the aubade, acerbic and badgering in contrast with the more conventionally tender poem discussed above. As Theodore Redpath points out, it might derive from Ovid's *Amores*, l. 13, which contains the cry, "*Quo properas, Aurora? mane!*" Whereas a tag such as 'Sunrise' would have had a purely temporal reference, "The Sunne Rising" allows for a transferred sense of 'the sun getting out of bed', and with much participial fuss to boot. This irreverence also pervades the hectoring start to the first stanza:

> Busie old foole, unruly Sunne,
>   Why dost thou thus,
> Through windowes, and through curtaines call on us?
> Must to thy motions lovers seasons run?
>   Sawcy pedantique wretch, goe chide
>   Late schoole boyes, and sowre prentices,
>   Goe tell Court-huntsmen, that the King will ride,
> Call countrey ants to harvest offices;
> Love, all alike, no season knowes, nor clyme,
> Nor houres, dayes, months, which are the rags of time.

Donne's bluster derives part of its force from the appositive gathering of vocative phrases, so typical of insult, of indignation that mounts above coherence. (One example amongst many that come to mind is the syntax with which Kent insults Oswald in *King Lear*—"Thou whoreson zed! thou unnecessary letter!") Both in this sentence and that which follows, Donne programmatically inverts the syntax, so that the subject has to push through the interposing adverbial phrases to make contact with its verb, its dogged inexorability registered in the 'local' anaphora of "through" and "through" while the unnatural demand for consonance between external, and subjective lovers', time embodies itself in the anomic wrenching and transposition of the adverbial phrase "to thy motions" before the subject and verb—"lovers seasons run". With the ensuing imperatives, Donne as it were deflects the summons from the couple, casting it back in the teeth of the sun [. . . .] [A]nother sequence of nouns from "schoole boyes" to "King" furnishes a further image of the external world, conceived in "The Good-morrow" in geographic, here in social, terms. And, predictably enough, in contrast with this multiplicity, that enswathing leitmotiv of Donne's love, the adjective "all", occurs in a phrase very similar to one in "The Good-morrow"—here "Love, all alike", there "thou and I / Love so alike". To offset the containment of a relationship so complete as to admit of no temporal division, Donne ends his stanza with a ragged inversion ("no season knowes, nor clyme") and a jostling asyndetic catalogue of "houres, dayes, months", which, though crowding upward in order of scale, are none the less undercut by the deflationary adjectival clause that qualifies them. The triple negative "no . . . nor . . . Nor" delimits the permanence of love by inking out the random transience of time. Both here and in "The Good-morrow", then, we encounter not so much a tangible evocation of the love as a suggestion of its qualities by a system of definitive deletion. Unlike poets more centrally placed in the Petrarchan tradition (poets who expend their energies on sensory transcriptions of feeling), Donne is content to silhouette his emotional states simply through a few scissor strokes about their edges. Negative definition is as crucial to his poetry—the buoyancies of "The Sunne Rising" ought not to blind us to the essential seriousness of the love at its centre—as the systematic negations (anti-, if not un-Petrarchan) of Shakespeare's Sonnet cxxx, "My mistress' eyes are nothing like the sun" to that. (It is also, incidentally, this bias towards definition rather than evocation that distinguishes the Metaphysical from the Petrarchan conceit, for the ingenuity so essential to the first leads it to eschew charged images and archetypes and to align such emotionally rebarbative items as compass-legs and coins to the most poignant of feelings.) The spirited impudence of "The Sunne Rising" likewise overturns the archetypal solemnities of the sun image as a *contre rejet* as the start of line 11 makes clear:

> Thy beames, so reverend and strong
>   Why shouldst thou thinke?
> I could eclipse and cloud them with a winke,

But that I would not lose her sight so long:
   If her eyes have not blinded thine,
   Looke, and to morrow late, tell mee,
Whether both the 'India's of spice and Myne
Be where thou leftst them, or lie here with mee.
Aske for those Kings whom thou saw'st yesterday,
And thou shalt heare, All here in one bed lay.

Donne seems at first to be offering us the adjectives "reverend" and "strong" in opposition to "beames" until, as we read on, we find them thrown back upon the sun in a supple-spined inversion.

—Rodney Edgecomb, "An Enquiry into the Syntax of Donne's 'The Good-morrow' and "The Sunne Rising," *English Studies in Africa* 25, no. 1 (January 1982): pp. 34–35.

ALFRED W. SATTERTHWAITE ON THE SEVEN SLEEPERS

[Alfred W. Satterthwaite is the author of *Spenser, Ronsard and Du Bellay: A Renaissance Comparison* (1960). In the excerpt below from his article "Donne's 'The Good-morrow,'" Satterthwaite discusses Donne's reference to the legend of the Seven Sleepers, focusing on their reawakening as a symbol of the radiant revelation granted to the lovers in this poem.]

Wherever John Donne's poem "The Good-Morrow" has been reprinted in modern times, whether in a collection of the poet's work or in an anthology, the fourth line of the poem ("Or snorted we in the'seaven sleepers den?") is usually given an explanatory footnote. A significant exception is A.J.C. Grierson's *Donne's Poetical Works* (Oxford, 1912), which makes no comment on the Sleepers in line 4, perhaps because the reference was obvious to Grierson in 1912. More recent editions, however, almost invariably supply a footnote. [...]

The contemporary reader is not expected to be familiar with the legend of the Seven Sleepers. The footnotes undertake to explain the reference with respect to its meaning in the context of the poem. But all the footnotes are unfortunately less than adequate. All of them describe the Sleepers as young Christians who were being persecuted by the Romans, who took refuge in a cave, and who slept more than 200 years; only one of them mentions that the sleepers eventually wakened. This is correct as far as it goes, but it does not go far enough. It provides a meaningful interpretation of the line in question, but it ignores the meaning of the line in the context of the whole poem.

To give the facts about the Seven Sleepers of Ephesus exclusively in terms of their sleeping a very long time is to ignore the most beautiful part of the legend, their awakening. The poem "The Good Morrow" is of course about sleeping, but it is still more importantly about awakening. The first stanza deals with the ignorance of sleep; the second and last stanzas deal with the radiant revelation that falling in love grants to the lovers, a quickening and an awakening. The first line of the second stanza reads: "And now good morrow to our waking souls."

Let us now turn to the legend of the Seven Sleepers of Ephesus, which is recounted in full by S. Baring-Gould, M.A. in his fascinating little book *Curious Myths of the Middle Ages* (London, 1888, pp. 93–112). There can be little doubt that the legend was known by Donne, for if he did not know it he would hardly have referred to it in a poem. It may very well be that John Donne, born and raised a Roman Catholic, was familiar with the full story of the Seven Sleepers in the *Legenda Aurea* of Jacques de Voragine, on which Baring-Gould based his account.

The legend tells of seven natives of Ephesus who had become Christians in the time of the Emperor Decius, who persecuted the new sect. They refused the imperial order to sacrifice to pagan idols, and fled the city, to hide in a cave on Mount Celion. Decius guessed that they were in a cave, and ordered that it be blocked with stones. Three hundred and sixty years later an Ephesian who was building a stable took the stones as construction material and thus opened the mouth of the cave.

The sleepers awakened, under the illusion that they had slept a single night. One of them, Malchus, left the cavern to seek food. He was bewildered to find a cross over the nearest gate to the city. Once in Ephesus, he was perplexed to hear people using the Lord's name when yesterday the name of Jesus had been proscribed. Malchus could not believe that the city was Ephesus. Upon asking a passer-by the name of the city and being assured that it was indeed Ephesus, "he was thunderstruck," says the legend.

At this point one may suggest that the lover in "The Good Morrow" finds himself thunderstruck in the second stanza as he bids good-morrow to his and his mistress' waking souls. To be in love as he is, is as marvelous, as splendid, as moving, and as incredible an awakening as for a persecuted Christian to awaken into a Christian world.

—Alfred W. Satterthwaite, "Donne's 'The Good Morrow,'" *Explicator* 34 (1976): 182, 184, 186.

[In his article "'The Good-Morrow' and the *Legend Aurea*," Misako Himuro discusses the reference to the "seaven sleepers" and focuses on its derivation from Donne's reading of William Caxton's *The Golden Legend* (1483), a reading which is supported by Donne's Roman Catholic upbringing.]

John Donne's 'The Good-morrow' is built on the lovers' awakening from their past puerile state into a life of true reciprocal love. The dramatic impact of the title is great: it suspends readers until they come to a full understanding at the beginning of the second stanza, 'And now good morrow to our waking soules', which concludes the preceding metaphorical remark about their former state, 'Or snorted we i'the seaven sleepers den?'

'The seaven sleepers' requires an annotation for modern readers. Herbert Grierson is mute in his edition of *The Poems of John Donne* (1912), but Helen Gardner gives the gist of the legend of the Seven Sleepers of Ephesus:

> Under the persecution of Decius seven noble youths took refuge in a cave where their pursuers walled them up to starve to death. A miraculous slumber fell upon them which lasted 187 years.

She also refers to 'the close of chapter xxxiii of Gibbon's *Decline and Fall*' for the source of this miracle, and Gibbon in turn informs the reader how the legend came to be translated from the Syriac by Gregory of Tours before the end of the sixth century, and how the story became widespread both in Christendom and in the Mohammedan world. [...]

Their attention is diverted to their physical need almost immediately after their awakening. Is it possible to obtain more details about their significant emergence from a long period of unconsciousness? The *Legenda aurea*, compiled by Jacobus de Voragine roughly 700 years later, satisfies this enquiry. Voragine's description characteristically is far more colourful and detailed. [...] Here, on their awakening, they first exchange greetings and then direct their thought to their past and future, just as the speaker of 'The Good-morrow' does. '*Se invicem salutantes*' strongly suggests an etiological link between Voragine and Donne.

William Caxton's rendering of this passage in *The Golden Legend* (1483) is as follows:

And it happened that of adventure the masons . . . opened this cave. And then these holy saints, that were within, awoke and were raised and *intersaluted each other*, and had supposed verily that they had slept but one night only, and remembered of the heaviness that they had the day before. And then Malchus, which ministered to them, said what Decius had ordained of them, for he said: We have been sought, like as I said to you yesterday, for to do sacrifice to the idols, that is it that the emperor desireth of us.

(emphasis added)

While the *Legenda aurea* was among the books most frequently reprinted between the years 1470 and 1530, *The Golden Legend* was Caxton's most popular publication which ran into as many as nine editions by 1527. Donne's upbringing was Roman Catholic, so that he would likely know The Golden Legend rather better than his Protestant coevals. In view of all this, it seems highly probable that the immediate source of his knowledge of the Seven Sleepers was either the *Legenda aurea* or its English version by Caxton.

—Misako Himuro, "'The Good-morrow' and the *Legenda aurea*," *Notes and Queries* (June 1993): 177–79.

D. C. ALLEN ON THE HISTORY OF THE MANDRAKE ROOT

[In the excerpt below from his article "Donne on the Mandrake," D. C. Allen provides a classical and biblical history of the mandrake root as used in "Go and Catch a falling star."]

In 1912 Grierson glossed "Get with child a mandrake root" with a not very helpful extract from *Vulgar Errors* on the man-shape of the root. This annotation was taken over, forty-four years later, by Redpath, who remarks that since not all mandrake roots resemble the male torso, one must avoid the "additional idea here of the impossibility of a male begetting a child on a male." It is, consequently, a good moment to consider what Donne meant by this line, and we are grandly informed by the four stanzas on the mandrake in "The Progresse of the Soule," stanzas elucidated in Grierson's edition by reprinting the passage from Sir Thomas Browne.

The migrant soul, Donne sets it down, flees from the apple when it is plucked by Satan and offered to Eve, and "in a Plant hous'd her anew." The plant forces its way through sparse soil, spreading east and west,

> Grew on his middle parts, the first day, haire,
> To show, that in loves businesse hee should still
> A dealer bee, and be us'd well, or ill:
> His apples kindle, his leaves, force of conception kill.

A complete description of "this quiet mandrake" which repeats the botanical narratives of Pliny (25.13) and Dioscorides (4. 78) succeeds, and then the herbal house of the wandering soul is destroyed by Eve.

> No lustfull woman came this plant to grieve,
> But 'twas because there was none yet but Eve:
> And she (with other purpose) kill'd it quite;
> Her sinne had now brought in infirmities,
> And so her cradled child, the moist red eyes
> Had never shut, not slept since it saw light;
> Poppie she knew, she knew the mandrakes might,
> And tore up both, and so coold her childs blood.

The whole history of the May apple is here. [. . .]

According to Greek *Physiologus,* the elephant, cold by nature must first eat of the mandrake when he wishes to beget young. To this end the elephant leads his mate to the neighborhood of Eden where this plant grows. First she eats; then he. The two elephants, the Greek text continues, are symbols of Adam and Eve who fell through eating the mandrake. [. . .] The legend of the elephants and the mandrake, with its very special meaning for Christians, got a wide currency though on some occasions, as in the *Bestiaire* of Phillippe de Thaün, the elephants eat "mandragora," whereas Adam and Eve eat "le fruit del pumier." Here we have a neat point, I think, that explains why Donne's Soul leaves the apple of temptation and takes refuge outside Eden in the mandrake.

We know that Eve ate an apple because the Vulgate tells us so—not in Genesis, but in Song of Songs (VIII: 5). [. . .] The Greek text keeps the appletree but says nothing about the corruption of "your mother"; the Hebrew and the English texts agree with it. But in all the texts the mandrake is close to the appletree. In VII: 13, the "Church" proposes that she and her "Spouse" go out to the vineyards where there are tender grapes and budding pomegranates; here at her gates, she remarks, are her love and fruits which she has laid up for her Lover.

—D. C. Allen, "Donne on the Mandrake," *Modern Language Notes* 84, no. 5 (May 1959): pp. 393–96.

James S. Baumlin on the Sun's Paradoxical Nature

[James S. Baumlin is the author of *Ethos: New Essays in Rhetorical and Critical Theory* (1994). In the excerpt below from his book *John Donne and the Rhetorics of Renaissance Discourse,* Baumlin discusses the paradoxical nature of the sun and the speaker's ambivalent responses in "The Sunne Rising."]

On the surface, much of this is suggestive of "The Good-morrow," where "love, all love of other sights controules, / And makes one little roome, an every where" (10–11). Elaborating upon this same trope, "The Sunne Rising" goes so far as to command the sun to "Shine here to us, and thou art every where; / This bed thy center is, these walls, thy spheare" (28–30). Initially, then, both "The Sunne Rising" and "The Good-morrow" declaim against time, both the time wasted before their discovery of love and the movement of time that threatens to separate the lovers, ending their pleasures (of course, the sun is traditionally an unwelcome guest in the genre, a "spy" that brings the lovers' typically adulterous relation to light). But where they diverge markedly from the medieval alba is in their claim to triumph over temporality, turning their rhetoric from the traditional complaint or lament to one of celebration.

In "The Sunne Rising," for example, the sun is reduced to a large cosmic alarm clock, calling the poet back to the daylight world of education, business, and politics; its task is no more than to "chide late schoole boyes, and sowre prentices" (5–6), reminding "countrey ants" of their "harvest offices" (8) with the same officiousness that it tells "Court-huntsmen, that the King will ride" (7). And yet the poet denies that the sun has power to control the lovers' lives, the very juxtaposition of "Court-huntsmen" and "countrey ants" suggesting how little he values the world of business and courtly ambition, the world he has left for love. The poet thus rejects the conventions of this genre at the same time that he repudiates his own initial arguments: no longer chided for invading the lovers' privacy, the sun is now welcomed into their world as a benevolent presence, bearing witness to their love and gracing their bedroom with its splendor. In his address to the sun, then, the speaker of "The Sunne Rising" can answer his own chiding question—"Must to thy motions lovers seasons run?" (4)—with a resounding no, for "Love, all alike, no season knowes, nor clyme, / Nor houres, dayes, months, which are the rags of time" (9–10). But in claiming to triumph over time, such lyrics more than diverge from convention; they must also, if implicitly, make a unique and perhaps perilous claim for the strength of their incarnationist rhetoric—and their success, or failure, to enact their form must rest upon such claims. Rajan, for one, finds at the heart of "The Sunne Rising" an implicit (if naïve) belief in "the alchemy of language," one that "can actually transform the world of fact represented by the motions of the sun, and create through rhetoric what cannot be affirmed through logic. That the extravagant hyperbole of the poem asks to be resisted is fairly obvious." It might not be so obvious, actually: such a poem invites our assent, invites us, in fact, to participate in its verbal transvaluation of reality at the same time that it invites our skepticism, our questioning whether such world-building magic is ever more than verbal shamanism. As Murray Krieger observes,

> The poetic gesture as love's gesture may transform the world's ways and its language, but not without undoing them. In its consummations it wins its eschatological victories for the poet-lover, though its reality-bound antagonists—wielding difference, distance, and death—are hardly dissolved. . . . If we are asked to believe in such magic, it is with the tentativeness and skepticism which even a poet-magician like Prospero acknowledges at the close of *The Tempest*.

Thus Krieger alludes to the play between divergent rhetorics, between public celebration and silent, transcendent meditation, between skepticism and the word-magic of sophism, all meeting in the miracle/illusion of poetic language. And the reader is left, finally, to choose. Whatever the rhetoric he or she chooses to read by will surely help regulate and systematize the interpretation (giving the interpretation itself, by the way, a greater unity and univocity than the poems themselves could ever possess).

—James S. Baumlin, *John Donne and the Rhetorics of Renaissance Discourse* (Columbia, Missouri: University of Missouri Press, 1991): 302–303.

CLAY HUNT ON "THE SUNNE RISING" AND "THE CANONIZATION"

[Clay Hunt is the author of *Lycidas and the Italian Critics* (1979). In the excerpt below from his book *Donne's Poetry,* Hunt compares "The Sunne Rising" with "The Canonization," noting that while both share such characteristics as an explosive beginning which is later tempered to romantic passion and both conclude with a portrait of lovers withdrawn from the world, "The Sunne Rising" banishes the ravages of time and is, instead, a poem of "youthful exuberance."]

There is, finally, one other fact about "The Canonization" which opens up an interesting possibility for speculation—the striking resemblance which it bears to "The Sun Rising." That poem, which is a more open and much less intricate piece of work, was probably written earlier than "The Canonization," and I see no reason to connect it with Donne's love for Anne More. But both poems are built on the same strategic plan: they begin with explosive brusqueness, as the lover tells an intruder on his love to get away and leave him alone, and they then modulate to an expression of sustained romantic passion. Both start, also, with a sharp realistic picture of what other people are doing—a semi-satiric survey of types of worldly ambition which is intended to suggest the normal concerns of life in the World, a world that the lovers have chosen to renounce—and they conclude with a picture of the lovers withdrawn from that world and completely absorbed in the contemplation of one another. Furthermore both develop an ingenious argument to prove that the world has been well lost for love because the two lovers have found the whole world in each other. But, along with these similarities, the two poems show fundamental differences. There are no gray hairs in "The Sun Rising": the lover in that poem is young, as one sees from his initial annoyance at the sun as an "old fool" and from his later patronizing condescension toward the sun's old age ("thine age asks ease"). His love, moreover, seems a matter of mere physical rapture, uncomplicated by intellectual analysis and without any suggestion of spirituality. And after the similarly theatrical opening stanzas, "The Sun Rising" develops a tone which is very different from that of "The Canonization." It is a poem of youthful exuberance and unclouded high spirits, a dramatic expression of the exultant brag of a young lover after a night of love.

I think Donne could hardly have failed to notice the similarities in theme and literary method between the two poems, and I doubt that the resemblance between them is accidental. It seems probable that when Donne decided to write, in "The Canonization," a poem justifying the loss of the world for love, he thought back to an earlier poem which he had written on the same theme, a poem expressing a very different state of mind and dealing with what he would see at this time as a very different kind of love, and that he took that poem as his artistic model. Probably he had already reworked the genre of "The Sun Rising," as well as the theme of the world well lost, in "The Good-Morrow," and I think he may have decided to rework "The Sun Rising" again, this time more closely, in "The Canonization." [. . .]

But if he did see the two poems as a matched pair, was the impulse which led him to play them off against one another nothing more than an interest in an abstract pattern of artistic contrast? If I am right in my belief than Donne was moved to write "The Canonization" by the pressure of his personal distress in the years following his marriage, and by a personal need to justify, not only to others but to himself, the loss of the world for his love, then it seems likely that Donne thought of "The Canonization" as "The Sun Rising" rewritten by an older, a sadder, and a wiser man.

—Clay Hunt, Donne's *Poetry: Essays in Literary Criticism* (New Haven: Yale University Press: 1954): 91–93.

JOHN CAREY ON DONNE'S RESPONSE TO COURT LIFE IN "THE SUNNE RISING"

[John Carey is the author of *William Golding: The Man and His Books: A Tribute on His 75th Birthday* (1987). In the excerpt below from his book *John Donne: Life, Mind and Art*, Carey discusses the relevance of Donne's strong emotional response to the courtly life which he both coveted and disdained in the poem "The Sunne Rising."]

In 'The Sunne Rising' Donne's claim to this royal status is placed resplendently at the poem's heart. [. . .] The phrase 'Busie old foole' reminds us of the 'busy fooles' in 'To his Mistris Going to Bed'; and as the girl in that elegy became America, so this one becomes the East and West Indies. The contempt and arrogance of the elegy persist here; but in commenting on this poem critics have rightly drawn attention to the misgivings which appear, like cracks, in its regal surface. Though emphatic about the all-eclipsing eminence of himself and the girl, Donne seems irascibly conscious of the rest of the world going about its business. What the real court and the real king may be doing stays at the back of his mind, and as if to counteract this the poem evolves its announcement of personal kingship. We remember how ardently Donne wanted, in actual fact, to be 'busie'; how useless he felt in his unemployment, like a spider in a window; how important he thought it to be integrated into the world and the court. The poem's first word has jealousy and resentment in it, as well as contempt.

Donne's vaunting language is, like all vaunting language, an expression of insecurity, and this makes the poem even more human. The pretension to kingship that he voices amounts to an acknowledgement of personal insufficiency. That the love of two ordinary, private people might be supremely significant is, we realize, a claim too assured for him to risk. When he tries to formulate it, he finds himself challenging comparison with kings, and to do this is to accept the conventional scale of values, with kings at its top, which he had seemed to be subverting. If lovers can be supreme only by being called kings, then kings are still supreme. The private world is valued only as it apes the public.

When Donne took holy orders he again felt the need to pretend, in his poetry, that the step had made him a king, or super-king. The poem 'To Mr. Tilman after he had taken orders' tells the newly ordained clergyman about the splendor of his, and Donne's, calling:

> What function is so noble, as to bee
> Embassadour to God and destinie?
> To open life, to give kingdomes to more
> Than Kings give dignities . . . ?

We recall, on reading this, that what Donne had really wanted to be was ambassador to Venice, not to God and destinie. The self-aggrandizement of the lines is a form of consolation. In making himself and Mr. Tilman seem noteworthy, the utmost that it occurs to Donne to do is to place them above kings and dignities they distribute. That would be enough to suggest how preoccupied he was with royalty, even if we didn't know that pursuing the dignities kings distribute had taken up most of his working life.

By comparison with the exhortations of 'To Mr. Tilman', the bid for royalty in 'The Sunne Rising' sounds vulnerable, and so more moving. It is noticeable that Donne changes his mind, in the course of the poem, about what he wants the sun to do. He starts by commanding it to go away, but when we reach the end we find that he wants it to stay with him and the girl and warm them. Until he mentioned it, we hadn't thought of them as needing to be warmed, and the idea is touching. The transition from dismissal ('goe') to invitation ('Shine here to us') in Donne's address to the sun is accompanied by a change of manner. The petulance of the opening gives place to conciliatory tone ('Thine age asks ease'). The speaker does not after all, it seems, want to be left alone with his love. Nor does he feel that they have, yet, enough pre-eminence. He wants the sun to shine on them alone. This shift in the poem's demeanour prevents it from settling into a piece of dead bravado. It has the instability of a living thing.

—John Carey, *John Donne: Life, Mind and Art* (New York: Oxford University Press, 1981): 108–09.

Donald L. Guss on the Renaissance Theory of Love

[Donald L. Guss is the author of *John Donne Petrarchist*. In the excerpt below from his book, Guss provides a summary of Renaissance love theory, a literary tradition which Donne resisted or otherwise sought to overturn in many of his poems.]

Because Donne is such a Petrarchist, I offer here a survey of Renaissance love theory. Since this theory has roots in Provençal poetry, and since Donne is sometimes thought to be a kind of stil-novist, I begin my survey early.

Courtly love theory—that is, doctrines in love poetry adapted to courtly tastes and manners—properly begins with the Provençal lyric. For the student of late-medieval intellectual history, Provençal love theory is fascinating. It reflects a new interest in the individual and his spiritual potentialities; and it is related to such movements as scholasticism, Christian Neoplatonism, and, perhaps, Arabic Neoplatonism. For the literary historian, however, Provençal poets and their imitators are important not for what they represent but for what they say. And their statements are fairly simple. Epistemologically, Provençal poets say that the lover perceives, imagines, remembers, and desires his lady. Medically, they argue that the lady's glance sends into her lover's blood a spirit which causes pallor, trembling, heats, colds, and stammering. Socially and rhetorically, they develop a code of behavior and a method of amorous persuasion. Though their epistemology and medicine fascinate these modern critics who hanker after obscure ideas, it is their manners and rhetoric which are of chief importance to the Provençal lyric, to Andreas Capellanus, and to the European tradition of courtly love.

Provençal love theory must be seen as it functions within the lyric. Generally, each lyric is located at a stage of adulterous love: the poet respectfully but passionately discovers to his lady his hitherto undisclosed love; or, after she hears his declaration favorably, he joyfully declares that he serves her proudly; or he ecstatically announces that he has been profusely rewarded by her ultimate favors; or with noble sorrow, he discloses that she has discourteously betrayed him. Within this context, the poet's emotions are intense, feudal, and idealized: burning like a moth in the flame of his lady's beauty and resurrected by her smile, he sings with joy of her sublime worth or with anguish of his hopeless desire. His reverence is reflected in his elegant, stylized language: he says that she is among other ladies like a rose among flowers.

The lady's praises, too, are delicate and passionate: she is exalted for her eyes, her greeting, and her elegant bearing—for her breeding, above all, which is called "knowledge," "wisdom," and "understanding." Her sublimity is revealed primarily by her amazing effects upon her poet, and by his reverent tone. Thus, Provençal poetry combines propriety with intensity. Its technique is esoteric, relying on aureate language, peregrine comparisons, and difficult meters. It is both impeccably courteous and intensely passionate.

Courtly love theory is essentially an ideal of amorous conduct and rhetoric within a feudal society (Capellanus' *De amore*, for example, is chiefly composed of model speeches for each caste of lover). Provençal literature reflects a taste for subtlety—for complicated rules and obscure instances (as in the "courts of love," social gatherings which as a pastime, dispute the proper course of conduct in difficult cases—often, probably, alluding to personal circumstances). In the lyric, however, the code of love is essentially a clear standard of propriety upon which the poet models himself, and to which he appeals when persuading, praising, or denouncing his lady (this last, generally, when she has been unfaithful). These are his principles: like contemporary courtiers, he accepts gentility as the highest social value; but he defines true gentility not by birth but by accomplishment and delicacy; he argues that love ennobles sentiments and inspires to worthy actions; and he concludes that since he loves so intensely as to be recreated by passion, he is worthy of his lady, no matter what her rank.

Upon this basis, the Provençal poet develops a feudal relationship between lady and lover; like a knight who serves a noble lord, the lover demonstrates his own nobility by his high-minded and worthy service; like the lord who accepts the worthy services of a noble knight, the lady is obligated to reward her servant. For moderns, it is worth emphasizing that thus Provençal love theory establishes a mutual obligation between lover and lady. The Provençal poet is elaborately courteous in invoking his rights, since they are consequences of his gentility: he requests as grace what is his in equity, refuses to insult his lady even after she has betrayed him, and faithfully serves his lady without reward. Throughout, he reflects the luster of a proud and noble courtesy. But beneath that luster is the mutual obligation between feudal lord and servant: the lover repeatedly indicates what courtesy requires of his lady, and continually reminds her that the good servant deserves his reward.

—Donald L. Guss, *John Donne Petrarchist* (Cambridge: Cambridge University Press, 1971): pp. 124–26.

Thematic Analysis of "Love's Alchymie"

"Love's Alchymie" is yet another poem contained within the volume *Songs and Sonnets*. The title contains the predominant conceit, absolutely necessary to understanding the complexity of the poem.

Alchemy was the chemistry of the Middle Ages and the 16th century which engaged in the pursuit of transforming baser metals into gold. It was, at the same time, caught up in the quest for the Elixir Vitae, a universal cure for all illnesses of the flesh, a concept that dates back to Plato. This medicinal metaphor derived from the Platonic tradition alludes to a cure for fever, thought to be caused by the restless unquietude of lust. It speaks of a spiritual balm, the sovereign remedy for sensuality. As a result, a link was forged between alchemy and spirituality.

However, at the same time the alchemist in literature is often characterized as an impostor prone to making bold claims; he is often a figure of satire and ridicule. In his play *The Alchemist*, Ben Jonson, a contemporary of Donne, described the alchemist as a "smoky persecutor of nature!" The alchemist has also been a symbol for the inherent dangers that accompany a journey beyond the limits of human knowledge, as in Marlowe's *Faustus* (published in final form in 1616), where the alchemist places himself far outside the boundaries of human understanding and salvation. "Regard his hellish fall, / Whose fiendful fortune may exhort the wise / Only to wonder at unlawful things."

Thus, by Donne's time, alchemy had accrued a long history which included conflicts between body and soul, the affirmation or sublimation of human sexuality, and the difficulties attendant upon separating divine truth from fraudulent illusion and deceptive rhetoric. With these various tensions in mind, we can begin to analyze Donne's agenda: bringing the "science" of alchemy to bear on his investigation of the nature of love. Donne assumed his contemporary audience would be familiar with alchemy and would understand his elaborate conceit.

The first stanza of "Love's Alchymie" sets up the conditions of the debate. The poet will take an oppositional stance to the practitioners of alchemy. Here, the alchemists have claimed to understand the mystery of love because they have ability to delve deeper into the unknown than ordinary humans can. "Some that have deeper digged love's mine than I, / Say where his centric happiness doth lie." Within these brief two lines are compacted the various tensions and multifaceted meanings within the alchemic conceit. As Clay Hunt has pointed out in his book *Donne's Poetry: Essays in Literary Analysis* (1954), "the image of 'digging for gold in a mine' suggests the arduous endeavor of the philosophic quest for a love whose essence is spiritual, and it implies the conventional Renaissance identification between gold and the human soul which forms the doctrinal basis for the central alchemy conceit. But from this image of a gold mine Donne develops further suggestions. . . . 'Dig' is a standard sexual term in Renaissance slang, and the coarse physical concreteness of that image is developed by a pun on the word 'centric,' which refers also to a woman's genitals" (36–37).

Furthermore, as in other poems, Donne's resistance to the courtly love tradition is once again highlighted. Here the unattainable woman has been transformed into an object of physical accessibility and anatomical scrutiny. Indeed, the language of love, which previously was highly refined and spoken by those of noble breeding, has now been relegated to the status of slang. Important social implications go along with that.

Donne, unlike the courtly lover who spent his passion lamenting the inaccessibility of his lady, admits that he has had several sexual experiences: "I have loved, and got, and told." And yet, for all that, he has not yet been able to fathom the secret nature of love. Indeed, Donne states that he will never be able to do so no matter how long he lives. "But should I love get, tell, till I were old, I should not find that hidden mystery." In fact, the poet now identifies with the plight of the alchemist who, although a deceiver of other human beings, is likewise a victim of his own misguided thinking. "O 'tis imposture all: / And as no chemic yet the elixir got, / But glorifies his pregnant pot."

For all their expenditure of physical and emotional energy, the poet and alchemist alike are left with nothing but extreme discomfort. They have nothing to offer but further deception, anything but an understanding of the nature of love. "So lovers dream a rich and long delight, / But get a winter-seeming summer's night."

In the second stanza, the poet returns to that discomfort, this time expressing the emotional and spiritual price paid for these fruitless questionings. Here he seems to dismiss the alchemy conceit. "Our ease, our thrift, our honor, and our day, / Shall we for this vain bubble's shadow pay?" Instead, the poet shifts his attention to the moral degradation of fulfilling lustful desires. He presents us with a jaded perspective on marriage as the institutional sanction for something which would otherwise be deemed immoral, an institution which we have no choice but to accept. "Ends love in this, that my man / Can be as happy as I can, if he can / Endure the short scorn of a bridegroom's play?" Because of this institutional restriction, marriage is a form of servitude that humbles the bridegroom who is forced to comply. Donne's lament for the degradation of the bridegroom leads to his bitter indictment of women and the courtly love tradition: "In that day's rude hoarse minstrelsy" (that is, the song of the roving troubadours, who sang of the lady's inviolable sanctity). "Hope not for mind in women; at their best / Sweetness and wit they are but mummy, possessed."

The punctuation in these final two lines are mostly the conjectures of modern editors, and where the commas are placed changes the lines' meaning to some extent. However, the implication is that women are little more than mindless flesh. The mummy image alludes to an illusion of a cure, which is actually only the preservation of death, not the elixir vitae that the alchemist promised. ❀

Thematic Analysis of "The Anniversarie"

In this poem from *Songs and Sonnets*, Donne once again, as in "The Sunne Rising" employs a political conceit, specifically that of the royal court and the status of kings. He uses this conceit to explore a personal relationship both in this world and the next, discussing the nature of subjectivity.

In the first six lines of the poem, the lover delivers what amounts to a dirge (a song of mourning or lament, sung during a funeral), as he likens the lovers' relationship to kings who, despite their pomp and circumstance, are vulnerable to the ravages of time; nature reigns supreme and even kings are subject to its vicissitudes. "All Kings, and all their favorites, / All glory' of honors, beauties, wits, / The Sun it self, which makes times, as they passe, / Is elder by a yeare, now, then it was / When thou and I first one another saw: / All other things, to their destruction draw."

Here, in remarking that the sun also grows older, the poet seems to want to subject nature to its own inconstancy, an inconstancy that serves as a backdrop to the relationship he portrays as unchangeable and far beyond the daily devastation of this world. "Only our love hath no decay; / This, no to morrow hath, nor yesterday . . . But truly keepes his first, last, everlasting day." In exalting their relationship as immune to death and decay, in contrast to all others—especially kings, who are incapable of escaping death's destructive path—Donne is subtly setting the lovers higher than sovereign rulers. Further, he creates an image of kings as the subjects of nature itself.

When Donne declares that nature itself is subject to its own fickleness, the sun now being a year older, Donne boldly overturns the conventional point of view that nature is eternal because it is forever dying and being reborn. The poet even more boldly declares that the span of time in which the sun grows old is measured by the lovers' relationship, thereby subjugating nature to a more powerful presence.

This stanza ends with a feeling of bravado over the death-dealing effects of time. When Donne spells the word *tomorrow* as two words—"to morrow"—he emphasizes this bravado, subtly suggesting that the poem's lovers have managed to rise above the divisions of time that mark the human experience. These divisions underscore the still greater separation between this world and the next, and yet the spiritual strength of the lovers' relationship transcends even this rupture in reality.

Nevertheless, the royalty conceit depends on a conventional recognition that kings are supreme and far above mere mortals, a convention Donne seeks to overturn in much of his poetry. Therefore, we are being subtly prepared for a reversal of the very same bravado that marks the beginning of the poem.

The next stanza tacitly acknowledges the presence of death: "Two graves must hide thine and my coarse, / If one might, death were no divorce." Here Donne introduces the anxiety that death will in fact physically separate the lovers—unless, of course, they were able to share a common grave. This anxiety is in sharp contrast to the self-assurance set forth in the previous stanza. Here, the poet acknowledges that royalty, a status he had predicted they had surpassed, is in the end vulnerable to death. He fears the same outcome for the lovers, whose power and prestige have dwindled in this stanza, for now he compares them to princes instead of kings: "Alas, as well as other Princes, wee." Furthermore, that decrease in power is highlighted when he places the comparison with royalty in parentheses: "(Who Prince enough in one another bee)," and their "royal" status becomes more self-consciously a rhetorical construct rather than a viable comparison. He had hoped this comparison would be "enough" for his beloved, but, like the punctuation marks that separate the lovers' "royal" status from those who at least can claim it politically, the kingship conceit shows itself to be simply a rhetorical construct, a self-deception destined to reveal itself.

That revelation becomes obvious when we are reminded that this poem is about persuasion, the lover trying to allay the fears of his beloved and ultimately his own. However, having acknowledged the physical reality of death and the ultimate separation of the lovers, that he "[m]ust leave at last in death, these eyes and eares," he is still able to compensate for the loss in a reaffirmation of the soul's immortality, the possibility of an increased love in the next world. "This, or a love increased there above, / When bodies to their graves, souls from their graves remove."

Once Donne establishes that his source of consolation is his belief in the eternal life of the soul, the next and final section of the poem returns to other aspects of his agenda: the reversal of the convention that kings are far superior to their subjects and a subversion of conventional notions of subjectivity. The stanza begins with a complete leveling of all distinctions between kings and their subjects ("And then wee shall be throughly blest, / But wee no more, then all the rest"). Daringly, the poet attempts to empower the lovers by denying any subjectivity or obligation to the King ("Here upon earth, we are Kings, and none but wee / Can be such Kings, nor of such subjects bee"). As part of this role reversal, the speaker is then able to assure his beloved that they need not fear treason for they are far beyond human reach and the vulnerabilities of mortal kings. "Who is so safe as wee? where none can doe / Treason to us, except one of us two."

However, the poet hints here that his agenda of supremacy and superiority can be undermined by the lovers themselves. Despite all his protests that their love is supreme above all other mortal considerations, the poem ends in doubt, tacitly acknowledging that it is a tentative argument at best, uncertain of its bold claims. The last stanza advises the lovers to be vigilant of their thoughts, paying careful attention to living their lives well. The lover then states that from "[t]rue and false feares let us refraine, / Let us love nobly, and live, and adde againe," for their true reign will take place in heaven. "Till we attaine / To write threescore, this is the second of our raigne."

For all its resistance to being held captive to conventional notions of time, the poem ends by recording its achievement according to those same temporal rules: the anniversary, which means a yearly return of some remarkable event. ❀

Thematic Analysis of "The Ecstasie"

In this next poem within *Songs and Sonnets,* the title itself suggests this is a complex poem. The word *ecstasy,* from the medieval Latin word *exstasis,* which meant to be taken out of place, has a very rich history. In the 16th century it had a pathological significance, for it was a word used to describe all morbid states of being which were characterized by unconsciousness. In Othello, Shakespeare's use of the word carried this meaning ["So, I . . . layd good scuses upon your extasie," (iv.1.80)]. Generally, in the 16th century a person who was ecstatic was in a state of frenzy or stupor accompanied by anxiety and fear. In a mystical sense, to be ecstatic meant to be in a state of rapture wherein the body became incapable of sensation, so that the soul might be engaged in contemplation of the divine. The word could also be a descriptive term applied to an outburst or tumultuous utterance. These multifaceted meanings are all necessary in order to appreciate the intricacies of this poem.

The common denominator among these various meanings of ecstasy is the idea of the body separated from the soul. At first this seems to run counter to one of Donne's fundamental goals: uniting the body with the soul in order to achieve wholeness. As we shall see, however, through a variety of conceits, both the body and the mind are actively engaged in establishing unity with the soul, and the ecstasy achieved in this poem is an affirmation of this union.

Thus, we are presented with a complete subversion of the original sense of the word *ecstasy.* That subversion is contained in the word *unperplex,* to become certain of some truth, to be clearly focused on one's thoughts and feelings rather than being rapturously transported to another place. As always for Donne, true spirituality can only exist when the body and soul have been inextricably linked; thus, this poem seeks to heal this rift, effecting an indissoluble bond between the bodies and souls of the two lovers. Both the regular rhyme scheme and the balance of four-line stanza help to promote the sense of harmony that is being sought.

The first three sections of the poem rely on reproductive metaphors, both human and vegetable, with the idea that propagation will bring a renewed strength and vitality. In the first section, where the two lovers recline on a bank of flowering violets, they form a sympathetic connection with the flowery bank. "Where, like a pillow on a bed, / A pregnant bank swelled up to rest / The violet's reclining head." Here, nature is in complete harmony with humanity, offering itself up as a healing balm.

Interestingly, violets were commonly used in medicines and confections, and their reoccurrence throughout the poem supports the recuperation that Donne actively seeks.

When we encounter the lovers in the next section of the poem, they are now tightly fastened to one another, so much so that their eyes are now woven together. "Our hands were firmly cemented / With a fast balm . . . Our eye-beams twisted, and did thread, / Our eyes upon one double thing." The vital connection between the lovers is through the eyes, which were conventionally considered the gateway to the soul. Thus, the foundation for a spiritual union has been forged.

In the next section, that physical union has produced an even stronger spiritual bond than either of them individually could have produced. Central to this conceit is the idea of grafting—affixing a part of one living thing upon another so as to form an even stronger species. "So to intergraft our hands, as yet / Was all our means to make us one." The word *graft* also has a surgical denotation, a process whereby a part of one living entity is transplanted onto another. This gives us a further extension of the healing powers of the violets. Donne seeks to correct the spiritual wrong that resulted from the body being torn from the soul. In fact, the sexual union has been commuted to the eyes, the site where this union takes place. "And pictures in our eyes to get / Was all our propagation."

The next two sections introduce another medieval concept, that of the psychomachy (conflict of the soul). The metaphor used to express this conflict is militaristic: "As 'twixt two equal armies Fate / Suspends uncertain victory." The outcome of this battle is uncertain: "Our souls . . . hung 'twixt her and me." This uncertainty creates a stupefying state for the lovers who are attempting to effect a peaceful resolution. This state implies one of the conventional meanings of ecstasy, but it is a nearly comatose state rather than one of supreme joy; the lovers are not in a state of blissful contemplation but in a state of arrested animation. "And whilst our souls negotiate there, / We like sepulchral statues lay." Thus, as he so often did, Donne overturns the traditional definition of a word.

The next two sections introduce the alchemy conceit in its most positive terms as a process of refinement, here understood as spiritual perfection. "If any, so by love refined / That the soul's language understood, / And by good love were grown all mind." Two things are important here: first, the lovers now possess a refined language that only the initiated have access to, just as the alchemist had to devise an esoteric language to express the arcane knowledge only a few could understand, and second, "good" love here means the achievement of spiritual knowledge or insight. The alchemy conceit continues with the souls of the individual lovers fused together as some new and powerful entity who is far greater than they were as two distinct souls. "He (though he know not which soul spake, / Because both meant, both spake the same) / Might thence a new concoction take, / And part far purer than he came." This union has lead to complete clarity and understanding ("This ecstasy doth unperplex") whereby they now understand true love as a result of the physical being joined with the spiritual. "We see by this it was not sex; / We see we saw not what did move."

In the next few sections, we return to the conceit of the violet as a propagating form of life that produces, through grafting, something greater than the original: "A single violet transplant . . . Redoubles still, and multiples." The violet's healing powers provide a visible example that the sum is greater than the parts. "When love with one another so / Interanimates . . . That abler soul . . . Defects of loneliness controls." Donne has thus presented us with the perfect loving relationship and, having established all that is necessary to the relationship, the poem now makes an abrupt shift, with the poet questioning why religious institutions have held firm sway over our way of thinking, causing us to blindly accept the destructive division between body and soul.

In the next few sections of the poem, the poet launches into an abrupt outburst, an outburst for that takes us by surprise, since the movement of the poem up to this point has been a steady progression toward harmony and inner peace. The poet catches us off guard and in so doing commands our attention. "But O alas; so long so far / Our bodies why do we forbear." He adeptly extends the ecstasy conceit to one of its peripheral meanings, a tumultuous utterance, which rails against that doctrine that would take from us what has rightfully been ours all along. "They are ours, though they are not we; we are / The intelligences, they the sphere."

This line of reasoning continues with the radical notion that we owe our bodies thanks for having brought us into the world. Donne asserts that those bodies themselves contain the means for improvement, an alloy being an impurity with the power to improve. "Yielded their forces, sense, to us, / nor are dross to us, but allay." With the acknowledgment that we enter this world imperfect while at the same time possessing the potential for future perfection, Donne advises us that our bodies are absolutely necessary to the soul's development; the body is a living text from which others may read and learn. "To our bodies turn we then, that so / Weak men on love revealed may look; / Love's mysteries in souls do grow, / But yet the body is his book." ✾

Critical Views on
"Love's Alchymie,"
"The Anniversarie," and "The Ecstasy"

N.J.C. ANDREASEN ON LOVE'S GRIM NATURE
IN "LOVE'S ALCHYMIE"

[N.J.C. Andreasen is the author of *John Donne: Conservative Revolutionary*. In the excerpt below from that book, Andreasen looks at "Love's Alchymie," paying special attention to Donne's grim view that love can bring neither happiness nor fulfillment.]

Loves Alchymie is a thoroughly grim, pessimistic, and despair-filled poem. Its power rests upon the paradox that the lover hates the lust which he feels and yet hates equally the naïve belief that love can be anything but lust. So, although he is thoroughly disillusioned by the false promises of joy which lust seems to offer, he decides to embrace the source of his disillusionment rather than believe a lie.

> *Loves Alchymie*
>
> Some that have deeper digg'd loves Myne then I,
> Say, where his centrique happinesse doth lie:
>   I have lov'd, and got, and told,
> But should I love, get, tell, till I were old,
> I should not finde that hidden mysterie;
>   Oh, 'tis imposture all [. . .]

This poem has obvious connections with *Elegie XVIII*, for it too maintains that love consists of digging for "the Centrique part." But *Loves Alchymie* also adds that digging for the centric part brings neither happiness nor fulfillment. Instead love offers only false promises, which are of two kinds, one described in the first stanza and the other in the second— fulfillment in physical union and fulfillment in love between minds. Sexual love is real, but it brings no satisfaction; spiritual love is not real and therefore can bring none either.

The lover begins by charging anyone who knows more about love than himself, who has "Deeper digg'd love's mine," to explain wherein consists its essential happiness. He himself has loved women, possessed them, and counted over his possessions; and yet his experience has only convinced him that, no matter how often he repeated it, he would never find any essential happiness in it. Love's joy is a mystery which will remain hidden from him forever or else, and more probably, it is simply an imposture like alchemy. No alchemist has ever found the *elixir vitae,* for which he continually searches and experiments, and no alchemist ever will, since it does not exist; yet the alchemist who accidentally produces some trivial thing which seems sweet-smelling or medicinally beneficial glorifies his alchemical vessels, alchemy, and himself. His accidental discovery is trivial, but the alchemist, ignoring the discrepancy between his expectations and actuality, makes himself happy by pretending that the inconsequential results of his labor are worthwhile. Lovers too pursue nonexistent joys; they dream of a "rich and long delight," and they pretend that the cold short pleasures of "a winter-seeming summer's night" are satisfying.

The speaker has, however, no doubt in his own mind about the extent to which the accidental joys of physical love can satisfy. He sees them as the shadow of a vain bubble; the theoretical essential joy of love (something more than mere lust) is as false as the elixir vitae—it is a vain bubble. The accidental joys of physical love which are acquired in pursuing the bubble are even more false, for they are only shadowy reflections of something which does not exist; shadows of real things are unreal enough, but the joys of physical love are as deceptively unreal as the shadow of a non-existent bubble. And yet, the speaker says, men sacrifice their ease, thrift, honor, and life for "this vaine Bubles shadow." It seems as if love is only lust, which is not worth the expense of spirit it demands. The speaker contemptuously notes that his own servant can acquire such amatory bliss by simply going through a marriage ceremony, can no doubt acquire it more cheaply and easily than he himself.

But despite the fact that the lover believes physical love to be unsatisfying and costly, he goes on in the concluding lines of the poem to assert that it is the only "love" possible. Harshly skeptical of Platonic love, he sardonically charges that anyone who is naïve enough to marry because he thinks he loves the lady's angelic mind is also sufficiently self-deceived to mistake the "rude hoarse minstralsey" of the marriage music for the music of the spheres. No one should hope to find mind in a woman; even at their best sweetness and wit, they are only physical creatures. And the love of women is nothing but lust, nothing but the possession of mummy (dead flesh used as a medicine), which leaves a bitter taste in the mouth but gives a temporary cure for the disease of lust.

—N.J.C. Andreasen, *John Donne: Conservative Revolutionary* (Princeton: Princeton University Press, 1954), pp. 120–24.

CLAY HUNT THE DEBATE BETWEEN BODY AND SOUL

[Clay Hunt is the author of *Lycidas and the Italian Critics* (1979). In the excerpt below from his book *Donne's Poetry*, Hunt discusses "Love's Alchymie" as a demonstration of Donne's debating skills, most particularly the debate between body and soul, with the figure of the alchemist attempting to bridge that gap.]

In "Love's Alchemy," as in the two poems we have just examined, Donne is again taking a heterodox position: he is operating as a skillful debater who is attacking a lofty and widely accepted view of love. But here the role is a serious one, and more is involved than the mere game of playing Devil's Advocate. Wit is turned into sarcasm, and there is no time for comedy. The poem is a tense and bitter expression of disillusionment.

The subject of "Love's Alchemy" is the same as that which lies behind both the facetious antics of "The Indifferent" and the metaphysical acrobatics of the conclusion of Elegy 19: the problem of the nature of love; and the poem is another document in that Debate between the Body and the Soul, between two philosophically antithetic conceptions of love, which was centered on the doctrines of Renaissance Platonism. But "Love's Alchemy" reflects a so much stronger emotional engagement with Platonic doctrine then we see in the Elegy that it may be well to pause for a moment to investigate why the question of the essential nature of love could seem a matter of such consequence to a thoughtful man of the Renaissance, with implications which extended beyond mere problems of psychology or of a code of personal behavior.

In the loosely integrated body of ideas from classical metaphysics, the Neo-Platonic Schools, and patristic and scholastic theology which made up the intellectual heritage of the Renaissance, the experience of human love was regarded, among other things, as an analogue of that act by which God had reconciled the warring elements in Chaos and created the order and beauty of the cosmos. Earthly love was conceived also as an analogue of religious experience. Since love was thought of in scholastic theology as the proper expression of the faculty of Will in the soul, human love could be seen as simply a lower manifestation of that latent impulse which impelled every soul to seek a direct relation with its Maker, an impulse which, in its higher, more spiritualized forms, shaded over into religious devotion and into transcendental intuition. To feel the spiritualizing influence of love was therefore, according to the Platonists and the Christian mystics, to undergo an experience by which man might penetrate into the hidden mysteries of the universe and arrive at his proper orientation in it. [. . .]

"Love's Alchemy" was written for readers who were familiar with the contemporary discussion of the pros and cons of Platonic doctrine and who would recognize that doctrine as the most widely held and most philosophically respectable contemporary theory of love. The whole pattern of thought in the poem, as well as much of its imagery, derives from the literature of Renaissance Platonism, and Donne expects his readers to understand the significance which these literary materials would have in their original context. He enters the debate in rebuttal against the Platonists, and his tactics are to seize on some devices in the opposing argument, turn them in his hands, and fling them back in his opponents' faces. The argumentative maneuver which forms the basis for his poetic strategy is that of giving a new twist to the metaphor from alchemy which he uses as a central conceit for the poem. This metaphor was a Platonic tag, since the analogy between alchemic research and spiritual love was a commonplace of Renaissance Platonism. In this poem Donne starts his attack by accepting, for purposes of argument, the validity of this analogy; and he proceeds, then, to explore still further aspects of the parallel between alchemy and Platonic theory, driving the analogy with a relentless imaginative logic which beats Platonic theory into the ground.

The logical points of departure for Donne's rebuttal are the normal implications which the Platonists had developed from this conceit. We can see those implications from the orthodox, essentially conventional treatment of the analogy in Sir John Davies' "Orchestra":

> [Love] first extracted from th'earth-mingled mind
> That heavenly fire, or quintessence divine,
> Which doth such sympathy in beauty find
> As is between the elm and fruitful vine;
> And so to beauty ever doth incline:
> Life's life it is, and cordial to the heart,
> And of our better part, the better part.
>
> This is true Love, by that true Cupid got . . .

Here love is likened to alchemy, first, because it is a process of spiritualization. Since the power of "true love" enables lovers to pass beyond sensuality to spirituality and thus to release the pure essence of their souls ("our better part") from the gross material encumbrance of their bodies ("th'earth-mingled mind"), love is analogous to the process by which the alchemist extracts the "quintessence"—the essence of gold, or "soul" of matter—from the base elements of "earth." But the phrase "cordial to the heart" in Davies' lines glances at another stock implication of the alchemy conceit in Platonic literature, an implication drawn from alchemic medicine. In the "New Physic" of Paracelsus, which was enjoying a vogue in England around 1600, the alchemist's quintessence, the *Elixir Vitae*, was supposed to be a medicine (a "cordial") which was a panacea for all the ills of the flesh. Since poets writing in the Platonic tradition often used the stock metaphor of a fever to suggest the restless inquietude of lust, and presented rational or spiritual love as a balm or sovereign remedy for the fleshly disease of sensuality, the medicinal powers attributed to the alchemist's Elixir provided them a basis for a further analogy between alchemy and spiritual love.

> —Clay Hunt, *Donne's Poetry: Essays in Literary Criticism* (New Haven: Yale University Press, 1954): pp. 33-36.

ARTHUR F. MAROTTI ON THE REJECTION OF COURTLY LOVE IN "LOVE'S ALCHYMIE"

[Arthur F. Marotti is the author of *Texts and Cultural Change in Early Modern England* (1997). In the excerpt below from his book *John Donne, Coterie Poet,* Marotti discusses "Love's Alchymie" as "a renunciation of love lyric" which makes a political statement, namely a rejection of "courtly striving."]

Despite his exercises in the mode, Donne portrayed fashionable amorousness as a cynical game in two lyrics probably composed about this time, "Loves Alchymie" and "Farewell to Love." A.J. Smith suggests that the latter "was written before the great celebrations of mutual love—while that further possibility, unglimpsed here, was yet to prove.... We must take it as a report on experience up till then; and this indeed seems to be how Donne himself saw it." It is useful to examine these renunciation-of-love lyrics, as Smith does, against the background of intellectual and literary history against which they were written and in the framework of Donne's other love poetry, but we should also recognize that poems like "Loves Alchymie" and "Farewell to Love" were also familiar political gestures. At least from the time of Wyatt, the renunciation lyric expressed disappointment and disillusionment with the game of courtly striving. This kind of poem, then, could be seen as an anti-courtly act on the part of the man whose ambitions were frustrated and who had mixed feelings about entering the courtly world. Both of Donne's lyrics are palinodes. At the end of *Cynthia's Revels,* Ben Jonson arranges for the stupidly fashionable courtier-lovers to be punished by being forced to sing a palinode—obviously the sort of verse that could be conceived of as the antithesis of the courtly amorous lyric and, therefore, by his comic logic, as a way of curing the characters of their foolish behavior. As in the case of the antagonist in Donne's fourth satire, what is wrong with the Court is symbolized by its amorous fashions. To reject these is to reject the rules they enacted and the environment to which they belonged.

Donne's two palinodes are exercises in an established form performed for an audience of sympathetic, knowledgeable males, gentleman-amorists, like his earlier Inns-of-Court readers, expert in the full range of libertine and polite love practices and able to entertain a critical point of view toward their own actions. These poems, like Donne's earlier amorous lyrics, are the work of a young man—mischievous, iconoclastic, self-consciously witty—yet they are presented also as the utterances of someone with considerable experience, particularly in the world of the Court where Petrarchan and Neoplatonic conventions were part of a system of deferential politeness, of patronage relationships, and of ambitious striving. As in the fourth satire and some of the verse letters of the late nineties, Donne dissociates himself from courtly practices and language partly in order to proclaim his independence and autonomy, partly to express frustration and disillusionment and he assumed a readership whose attitudes and awareness were similar to his.

The blunt rhetorical manner of "Loves Alchymie" marks it, like the libertine elegies and lyrics, as a male-audience piece. Through the use of the first-person-plural pronoun in the poem's second stanza, the first stanza's personal disenchantment becomes a kind of shared cynicism. This lyric assumes that speaker and listeners have both acted the role of the fashionable lover, wasting their "ease," "thrift," "honor," and "day." The contemptuous dismissal of marriage in the poem resembles the comic hostility to the institution expressed in some of the love elegies, and the critique of the courtly Neoplatonic amorist's attitude toward love looks like the easy gesture of the libertine skeptic. Like some of the earlier lyrics and some of the prose pieces of the nineties, this poem is an exercise in outrageous paradox, deliberately excessive in its statements in order to force a hard reexamination of its subject matter.

"Loves Alchymie" particularly mocks the Neoplatonic "loving wretch" who views love as a spiritual or mental joining, the path to a "hidden mysterie." Donne uses a kind of facile antifeminism (e.g., "Hope not for minde in women") to demythologize the *donna angelicata* of spiritual lovers, perhaps with a contemporary sonnet sequence like Spenser's *Amoretti* in mind. The cynicism of the piece is far-reaching: it not only criticizes the foolishness of some forms of fashionable loving, but also the experience of love in a more general sense. To claim "'tis imposture all" is to reject the good with the bad, the sensible with the foolishness. The end of the first stanza has the tone of personal disappointment, if not of self-hate: "lovers dreame a rich and long delight, / But get a winter-seeming summers night." Expressing skepticism about finding "happinesse" in love, either through fashionable amorousness or marriage, the poem seems more than a mere literary experiment in desentimentalization. It seems to speak for a shared discontent.

—Arthur F. Marotti, *John Donne, Coterie Poet* (Madison, Wisconsin: The University of Wisconsin Press, 1986): pp. 110–12.

N.J.C. ANDREASEN ON IDEAL LOVE IN "THE ANNIVERSARIE"

[N.J.C. Andreasen is the author of *John Donne: Conservative Revolutionary*. In the excerpt below from that book, Andreasen discusses "The Anniversarie" as a representation of the lovers' relationship which is ideal because it is outside the realm of time and change. Donne's argument for ideal love, says Andreason, is based on the lovers' being in a state of grace.]

The Anniversarie is another testimony to the practicality of idealistic love, especially to its security and endurance. Here a lover celebrates the first anniversary of his love by composing a poem addressed to his lady, and his anniversary gift to her rejoices that although a year has passed by, the love which they share has not been touched by time. His poem is built upon contrasts between the mutable and the permanent, the worldly and the otherworldly, the dynamic and the static; in spite of the pervasive presence of decay, fickleness, and change in the earthly world, he and his lady have achieved a love which thrives in the world but is free of earthly mutability. [. . .]

As the poem begins the lover looks around the universe, observing the transiency to which all things seem to be subject. As he lists them with slow stately periodicity, building to the statement that in changing all things are also drawing to their own destruction, he is recognizing the mortality of earthly delight, glory, and pleasure. The power of Kings and the privileges of their favorites will not last. Nor will more hard-won favors that man enjoys—"honors, beauties, wits." Even the source of time, the sun itself, is subject to its own self-created tyranny of transiency. Dynamic decay seems everywhere, but the lover turns from this *contemptuous mundi* strain to the one thing which can escape time's tyranny, the love which he and his beloved share. Paradoxically, although their love is also elder by a year, it is somehow both in time and outside of time, in the world but not of the world, for "Running it never runs from us away."

In the next stanza the lover admits that, although their love is not subject to destruction, their bodies will certainly die, be buried, and decay like all other earthly things. Not only will they die, but they will lie in two separate graves. Although his warning of *memento mori* does not seem the most appropriate anniversary gift, the lover, having been created by Donne, turns its incongruity into a triumph: because their love lives in their souls rather than their bodies, their separation through death will increase their love rather than diminish it. He looks upon death with confidence, seeing it as a test of their love, the outcome of which is not in doubt. Theirs are souls where nothing dwells but love, and after death, when their souls arise from their graves and ascend to heaven to meet God face to face, this love will prove itself. To love such as theirs, loss of the physical world is no very painful loss, for their love is built on a spiritual base rather than a physical one and thus will achieve an even greater fulfillment when placed in its natural surroundings. In heaven, the lover says in the next stanza, they will be thoroughly blessed, more blessed than they were on earth. For in heaven they will enjoy the companionship of others who are no more blessed then they and who share their joy and fulfillment; his genuine devotion to *caritas* is clear, for he casually assumes that the highest happiness arises from seeing others who are equally happy; on earth, although they are kings, there are no others around them who have achieved the same calm delight. Because they have not committed themselves to the transient Things of the World, therefore, they need not fear their treason and inconstancy. They have only one another to fear, and nothing to fear in one another.

The lover does perhaps sound as if he feels there is cause for fear when he says "True and false feares let us refrain," especially in the light of the preceding lines. But he speaks of *true* and *false* fears; the fear that one of them will do treason to the other is a false fear, and the true fears are those of the first and second stanzas, of mutability and separation through death. The lover is, in effect, saying "Since we have no reason to fear death, for heaven's sake let us avoid jealousy and suspicion while on earth." The poem is organized around the various temptations to fear which love must face: of decreasing with age and the passage of time, of loss of physical love through death, and of treason or dishonesty by one of the partners. Each is overcome. The Anniversarie expresses a state of grace in love, a love which brings faith and hope because it is built upon charity. [...]

In *The Anniversarie,* however, death and separation were only possibilities; the lovers faced them in theory, but not in actuality. But in other poems Donne imagines the response of lovers when threats of separation or death do become actualities. Because their love is founded on a lasting spiritual base, because it is tempered by a recognition of the facts of the universe, it submits to tests and trials successfully. In poems such as *A Valediction: forbidding mourning* or *A Feaver,* realistic idealism proves itself when faced by temptations to fear or to despair, when faced with separation, sickness, and death.

—N.J.C. Andreasen, *John Donne: Conservative Revolutionary* (Princeton: Princeton University Press, 1954): pp. 219–21, 223.

Arthur F. Marotti on Comic Elements in "The Anniversarie"

[Arthur F. Marotti is the author of *Texts and Cultural Change in Early Modern England* (1997). In the excerpt below from his book *John Donne, Coterie Poet,* Marotti discusses the comic elements in "The Anniversarie," a poem which he believes is addressed to Donne's wife and one of several poems which "celebrate the possibility of a constantly improving relationship."]

In amorous poetry love rivals are figuratively economic rivals; in society they were actually so. As in "The Anniversarie," the speaker pretends that the real danger to love comes from the "treason" of which the lovers themselves may be guilty, not from relevant external factors. The lover's claims of jealousy and possessiveness are facetious ones, the means of treating once again the topic of love's growth.

> Yet I would not have all yet,
> Hee that hath all can have no more,

And since my love doth every day admit
    New growth, thou shouldst have new rewards in store;
Thou canst not every day give me thy heart,
    If thou canst give it, then thou never gav'st it:
Loves riddles are, that though thy heart depart,
    It stayes at home, and thou with losing savs't it:
But wee will have a way more liberall,
    The changing hearts, to joyne them, so wee shall
Be one, and one anothers All.
         (23–33)

As the pun in the second line of this stanza suggests, this lyric was probably written for the woman Donne married. The comic economics of the poem is extended in this section into an argument for sexual union, a persuasion grounded in the morality of reciprocity through which the beloved can respond to the lover's "New growth" of love with "new rewards." Instead of requesting payment in kind, an increase in affection on her part, the lover mischievously suggests she must give him something else, since she has already granted her heart. In focusing in a teasing manner on the sexual union that would express their mutual commitment, the speaker discards both the Petrarchan framework of sighs and tears and the potentially troubling economic framework of the first two stanzas, as he uses the occasion to celebrate the fact that they are "one, and one anothers All." The chronology that this lyric implies—the ongoing history of mutual lovers who have given their hearts to one another, are worries about circumstances hostile to their love, but can look forward to a deepening of commitment—may be a fictional one, but it probably was well suited to the situation of Donne's relationship with Ann More in the stage following their formal pledge of mutual fidelity. [. . .]

Whereas poems like "Love's Growth" and "The Anniversarie" celebrate the possibility of a constantly improving relationship, "A Lecture upon the Shadow" depicts full, honest mutuality as a point of perfection from which the lovers can only "faint, and westwardly decline" (19). The final epigrammatic couplet suggests improvement and growth before the achievement of true reciprocity, but destruction the moment it begins to deteriorate: "Love is a growing, or full constant light; / And his first minute, after noone, is night" (25–26). As Louis Martz has remarked: "There is no comfort in this poem, only the presentation of a precarious dilemma. Love's philosophy, it seems, begins with the recognition of the shadow of decay." Donne, apparently, could not postulate a love removed from the world of time any more than he could forget that it was involved in a larger set of social relationships.

—Arthur F. Marotti, *John Donne, Coterie Poet* (Madison, Wis.: The University of Wisconsin Press, 1986): pp. 146–48.

JOHN CAREY ON THE LANDSCAPE OF
"THE ANNIVERSARIE"

[John Carey is the author of *William Golding: The Man and His Books: A Tribute on His 75th Birthday* (1987). In the excerpt below from his 1981 book *John Donne: Life, Mind, and Art*, Carey discusses the landscape of "The Anniversarie" as a "wreck of empires and solar systems" and compares the deeper anxiety of this poem, in which death will end the lovers' "supremacy," with the anxiety exhibited in "The Sunne Rising." Carey also discusses the contemporary audience to which the poem is addressed, an audience which shared Donne's veneration for the royal court.]

In this, and in its anxiety, it resembles another of Donne's greatest poems, 'The Anniversarie.' But whereas the lover of 'The Sunne Rising' worries about being left out in the cold, the lover of 'The Anniversarie' pits himself against the approaching dark:

>All Kings, and all their favorites,
>   All glory'of honors, beauties, wits,
>The Sun it selfe, which makes times, as they passe,
>Is elder by a yeare, now, then it was
>When thou and I first one another saw:
>All other things, to their destruction draw,
>   Only our love hath no decay;
>This, no tomorrow hath, nor yesterday,
>Running it never runs from us away,
>But truly keepes his first, last, everlasting day.
>   Two graves must hide thine and my coarse,
>   If one might, death were no divorce.
>Alas, as well as other Princes, wee
>(Who Prince enough in one anther bee,)
>Must leave at last in death, these eyes, and eares,
>Oft fed with true oathes, and with sweet salt teares;
>   But soules where nothing dwells but love
>(All other thoughts being inmates) then shall prove
>This, or a love increased there above,
>When bodies to their graves, soules from their graves remove.
>   And then wee shall be throughly blest,
>   But wee no more, then all the rest.
>Here upon earth, we'are Kings, and none but wee
>Can be such Kings, nor of such subjects bee;
>Who is so safe as wee? where none can doe
>Treason to us, except one of us two.

True and false feares let us refraine,
Let us love 'nobly, 'and live, and adde againe
Yeares and yeares unto yeares, till we attaine
To write threescore: this is the second of our raigne.

The first three lines of the poem, blending kings and glory with the sun, sound like a fanfare to majesty. But they are a dirge. the gorgeous blaze darkens, and the poet's individual claim springs clear of the dying splendours massed at the start. It is over the wreck of empires and solar systems that the first stanza strides forward.

Despite this brave beginning, anxiety goes deeper here than it did in 'The Sunne Rising,' and that poem's perkiness and banter have been stifled. Confidence caves in after the first stanza. As soon as the second begins, we can tell that a more concerned and perplexed voice has taken over, and though this voice tries to argue itself and the girl into putting a brave face on things ('Let us love nobly'), it admits that such courage is a mode of self-deception. There are 'True' as well as false fears, however determinedly one may 'refraine' from thinking about them; and the vision of the sexagenarian lovers in the last line doesn't, when dwelt on, carry much comfort.

The claim to kingship is less confident, too, than in 'The Sunne Rising.' Instead of being flung in the face of the facts—'She' is all States, and all Princes, I'—it is sidled into the poem as a piece of special pleading, while Donne comforts the girl about death. Aren't they, after all, he coaxes her to believe, 'Prince enough in one another'? That qualifying 'enough' betrays the pretence: they are not real princes. And though the third stanza takes a higher tone ('none but wee / Can be such Kings'), the effect is weakened by the need to prop it up with declamation ('Who is so safe as wee?').

But the fact that the poem's confidence gets eaten away doesn't mean that the wish to feel supreme grows less. Quite the contrary: the thought of death is alarming, we must observe, not because death will separate the lovers, or destroy their love, or diminish their happiness. None of these things, Donne persuades himself, will happen. It is alarming because death will end their supremacy. Dead, they will be totally happy ('throughly blest'), but no happier than 'all the rest' and that is unbearable. It is not happiness but superiority that Donne creates, which is why he hustles the afterlife out of his poem, and returns to his royal preeminence ('Here upon earth, we'are Kings'). He knows that their reign will be only temporary: the time fuse, as the last line tells us, is already burning. But he clings to their earthly reign nevertheless. And that represents a major change of direction in the poem; for at the start it was their disembodied love, free of time, knowing no tomorrow or yesterday, that Donne celebrated. Now it is their monarchy, measured in years.

Donne could, of course, have written a simpler poem if he had assumed that he and the girl would go on being kings after death. Then the need to choose between heavenly blessedness and royal supremacy would have been avoided. [...]

Donne was at times prepared to believe that there might be ranks and degrees in heaven. 'That there are degrees of Glory in the Saints in heaven, scarce any ever denied,' he remarked in a sermon of 1626. 'Heaven is a Kingdome and Christ a King, and a popular parity agrees not with that State, with a Monarchy. He wasn't always so sure. Only three years later, in another sermon, he took a different view: 'all shall rise alike . . . all that rise to the right hand, shall be equally Kings.' Even this egalitarian doctrine, though, would have allowed him to present his lovers, in 'The Anniversarie' as kings in heaven—for he plainly states that they will be among the blessed. But he didn't choose to. He planned his poem so that the frailty, as well as the supremacy, of the kingship it boasts should be exposed. He pitted love's kings against unkinging death, so that the poem's certitude should be tempered by doubt, its ambition by anxiety.

Although Donne's eagerness to acclaim the sovereignty of himself and his love is, in these two poems, clouded with doubts, it remains unmistakable. He was profoundly excited by the thought of majesty. To readers of liberal views, this might appear a blemish. Donne's equation of his love with kingship, such readers might object, links it with political power and possession. The girl may become the world ('all States'), but she is a world owned and ruled, indeed, rifled and exploited. She is 'both the 'India's of spice and Myne'. The same sort of reader would naturally be inclined to dismiss Donne's adulation of the great, and his eagerness for royal favour, as mere opportunism and greed. To understand this part of his mind correctly, however, we must appreciate that veneration for the court and for the grandees who peopled it was so deeply embedded among his imaginative and spiritual impulses that it became an element of his religious belief. If we think of the Renaissance as the epoch in which glorification of the court, and of the prince as earthly God, reached its apogee, then Donne was a Renaissance man in nothing more than this.

—John Carey, *John Donne: Life, Mind, and Art* (New York: Oxford University Press, 1981): pp. 110–12.

[Dwight Cathcart is the author of *Doubting Conscience: Donne and the Poetry of Moral Argument*. In the excerpt below from that book, Cathcart discusses "The Extasie," focusing on the status of the truth in the speaker's state of mind.]

"If it be truth," Taylor asserted, the believer will know it; yet casuistry arises, and the speaker begins to speak precisely because the "Lord's goods" are not immediately recognizable. Each time, in each special case, he must begin all over to search for and to define his truth. In no poem is this more true than in "The Extasie," whose very title seems to refer to an extraordinary way of knowing. [. . .] The speaker here is clearly concerned with showing that he has become "all minde" and that only by becoming so pure may he or anyone understand the truth expressed in "soules language." It is "by love refin'd," "by good love"—by these ways of knowing—that one comes to the knowledge of this "new concoction" which "doth unperplex / (We said) and tell us what we love" (ll. 29–30). The speaker then attempts a definition of that truth, concluding with easy assurance, "Wee then, who are this new soule, know, / Of what we are compos'd, and made" (ll. 45–46). *How we know* and *What we know* are two concerns of the poem, perhaps even the two major concerns, and the poem seems to be an essay at an epistemology for lovers. The "argument" over "The Extasie," whose history Helen Gardner has defined, may have resulted from a misunderstanding of the epistemology of the poem. The kind of truth the speaker seeks, and his necessary method of arriving at that truth may not have been recognized.

How we know for these two persons, at least in the first forty-eight lines, is by ways other than the rational. It is through a process of refinement of the soul as it purifies itself of the body: "Our soules, (which to advance their state, / Were gone out,) hung 'twixt her, and mee" (ll. 15–16). The precondition for knowing is just this going out of the soul from the body, and it becomes not merely prerequisite but method: "Wee see *by this*, it was not sexe" (l. 31; italics added). Even more clearly are the first forty-eight lines of the poem a definition of *What we know*. As the two lovers sit on the pregnant bank, they seek to "make us one" (l. 10), and what they learn in the ecstasy makes them one, even in their language: "Because both meant, both spake the same" (l. 26). The knowledge that they seek and that surely the speaker seeks is not knowledge of her or of him, not sex, not "what did move" (l. 32), but knowledge of what it is they create when they come together, a "new concoction" (l. 27), "Mixture of things" (l. 34), "That abler soule" (l. 43). It is a truth which is not grounded in any sensory experience; it is a truth out of two separate persons translated into a new soul "whom no change can invade" (l. 48). Nowhere is that truth which defines them in the ecstatic state related in any way to the world of the senses. What they know of themselves in these forty-eight lines is of themselves as they have "growen all minde" (l. 23).

The truth of the ecstatic state toward which they drive is not a truth which may be employed, and the poem as it stands down through line forty-eight is not didactic. These lines do not look beyond themselves and as truth have nothing to do with the affairs of men. They illuminate and purify but to no practical end; the force of the truth is not centrifugal but gravitational. Like mystical truth generally, the truth of the ecstasy seems to be inward looking and useless in application. If one must return from the ecstatic state, one can bring back with one only the memory of that truth, not the thing itself, and only by changing it can one make it change one's life. The effect of attaining such a truth is inevitably to be drawn back again and again deeper and deeper into the ecstatic state where alone the truth has validity. This mystical truth makes all else seem sepulchrous like the bodies on that bank, and its brilliance throws all else into deep shadows of insignificance. With its own special intensity, it makes other truths weak and denies the validity of other values. For those two on that pregnant bank, there seems for a time to be no other life but what they create invisibly between them.

Yet, as the poem seems to shift its emphasis and focus after line forty-eight, it refers to two separate and distinct needs for truth, the spiritual and the physical, and the truths defined in the poem seem to be of separate and contradictory things. The first forty-eight lines of the poem describe one thing and the final lines argue toward another, and the relation between the two remains unclear. The question in lines forty-nine and fifty amazes, and the last lines of the poem seem anti-climactic, a falling away at best, and, at worst, immoral.

—Dwight Cathcart, *Doubting Conscience: Donne and the Poetry of Moral Argument* (Ann Arbor: The University of Michigan Press, 1975): pp. 72–74.

[James S. Baumlin is the author of *Ethos: New Essays in Rhetorical and Critical Theory* (1994). In the excerpt below from his book, *John Donne and the Rhetorics of Renaissance Discourse*, Baumlin discusses "The Extasie" (and "The Canonization") as a poem which explores the problematic union of body and soul and the "subtle knot" that must be created in order to make that union binding.]

The diversity of human experience and the limited powers of language demand at the very least these two rhetorics, and many of Donne's lyrics (some of his finest, in fact: "The Canonization" and "The Extasie") arise out of their subtle interplay. Indeed, exploring the problematic unity of soul and body, of that "subtle knot, which makes us man" (64), "The Extasie" is no less than a poetic disputation on these competing theologies of language, for which reason we might turn now to this remarkable poem. St. Augustine provides the theological context: "the condition of man," he writes, "would be lowered if God had not wished to have men supply His word to men. How would there be truth in what is said—'For the temple of God is holy, which you are'—if God did not give responses from a human temple . . . ? For charity itself, which holds men together in a knot of unity, would not have a means of infusing souls and almost mixing them together if men could teach nothing to men." Though separate in the flesh, Christians partake of one spirit, that of charity, which provides a divine exemplar for the physical love that seeks, similarly, to mingle souls. And the means of this infusing or mingling (in fact the rhetorical foundation of this linguistic theology) has at once become dialogue in-the-flesh. For communication is a mode of communion, God (and man) speaking to man through the material human body; the preacher—and the lover, we might add—is thus entrusted with the task of carrying on the Incarnation, bringing charity to all, knitting men together in a "knot of unity." Is the sharing of words any less an act of love than the more physical sharing of "blood," say, or semen? It is, perhaps a greater sharing in that words are the lifeblood of the spirit; indeed, their reality is spirit. By means of its paradoxical "dialogue of one" (74), "The Extasie" thus seeks to defeat physical separation, raising participants to a level of consubstantiality, *psyche, eros,* and *logos* meeting in the space of the love poem.

The first six stanzas, one third of this relatively long lyric, describe a scene of erotic play and rhetorical as well as physical posturing between the lovers. But though joined physically by hands and eyebeams, they seem otherwise far from united, their only "propagation" being "pictures on our eyes" (11–12), and image that at once subtly questions the poet's incarnationist argument, pointing again to the disjunction between the real and the representation: while acts of love beget breathing human offspring, the love poet here, as in "A Valediction: of Weeping," begets but "pictures." Thus the early stanzas prepare for the lovers' physical union by the paradox of extasis, the very disembodiment of their souls (and a suspension, it would seem, not only of the souls but of incarnationism itself):

> As 'twixt two equal Armies, Fate
>   Suspends uncertaine victorie,
> Our soules, (which to advance their state,
>   Were gone out,) hung 'twixt her, and mee.
>
> And whil'st our soules negotiate there,
>   Wee like sepulchrall statues lay;
> All day, the same our postures were,
>   And wee said nothing, all the day.
>   (13–20)

Disembodied, the lovers "said nothing, all the day" (20), and apparent denial of physical speech. At the same time, however, the poet asserts the reality of "soules language," which only someone "so by love refin'd" would have "understood" (21–22)—or would simply be able to hear and, in hearing, bear witness to their love. The following lines, presumably, form the discourse such a lover would overhear:

> This Extasie doth unperplex
>   (We said) and tell us what we love,
> Wee see by this, it was not sexe,
>   Wee see, we saw not what did move:
> . . . .
> When love, with one another so
>   Interinanimates two soules,
> That abler soule, which thence doth slow,
>   Defects of lonelinesse controules.
>
> Wee then, who are this new soule, know,
>   Of what we are compos'd, and made,
> For, th'Atomies of which we grow,
>   Are soules, whom no change can invade.
>   (29–32, 41–48)

Though souls are "Th'intelligences" and bodies "the spheare" (52), nonetheless the body and soul form a complex unity, an inspirited material substance of "allay" (56). Human nature is itself inherently mixed, after all, the soul necessarily dwelling in the body, coming to know and love other souls through the body's senses. Love "interinanimates" the souls, then, creating an intersubjectivity or "dialogue of one."

And the body becomes the meeting place of these souls, the means through which "soule into soule may flow" (59).

—James S. Baumlin, *John Donne and the Rhetorics of Renaissance Discourse* (Columbia, Missouri: University of Missouri Press, 1991), pp. 202–205.

HELEN B. BROOKS ON EXEMPLARY LOVE

[In the excerpt below from her article, "'Soules Language': Reading Donne's 'The Extasie,'" Helen B. Brooks analyzes the poem as demonstrating an "exemplary love" for others to follow and states that that purpose is achieved through the "dialogue of one" in which the reader is actively engaged with the text.]

"To understand a metaphor," writes Stanley Cavell, "you must be able to interpret it; to understand an utterance religiously, you have to be able to share its perspective." This distinction, derived from Wittgenstein, speaks directly to understanding "The Extasie," given that the poem's meaning inheres in the reader's grasp of its epistemological bearing. The role of the reader in constituting meaning is not surprising when we recognize that the lovers' stated mission in the world is to reveal to "weake men" their exemplary love. I am proposing that Donne effects their revelation of love by making the verbal substance of their love, "this dialogue of one" (74), the content not only of the poem's discursive subject, but of its conceptual form as well. [. . .]

But the act of reading "The Extasie" should be distinguished from the conception of reading best described by Georges Poulet as the surrender of the self to the thoughts of the speaker: "I am on loan to another, and this other thinks, feels, suffers, and acts within me." Instead, "The Extasie" engages the reader in a constitutive relationship with the text by way of the silent, but implicitly responsive interlocutor. Because the interlocutor does not directly voice her thoughts, but whose presence nevertheless is implied by the single speaker's words, the reader is enlisted as the completing—and thus actualizing—agent of the two lovers' "dialogue of one."

This way of reading comes closer (though it is not identical) to Wolfgang Iser's conception of the dynamics of reading. Literary texts, according to Iser, are full of places of indeterminacy, of "gaps," and thus

"Whenever the flow is interrupted and we are led off in unexpected directions, the opportunity is given to us to bring into play our own faculty for establishing connections—for filling in the gaps left by the text itself." Iser regards the gaps in a literary text as that which draws the reader into a specific relation with the text, and by supplying "what is meant from what is not said," the reader "grasp[s] the pattern underlying the connections." In supplying the other side of the "dialogue of one," the reader of Donne's "Extasie" not only becomes essential to meaning, but occupies a plane of reality contiguous to the two lovers themselves. This vantage point, made possible by the silent interlocutor, grants Donne's readers immanent knowledge of the interrelationship between the speaker and the silent interlocutor. So that like the two lovers, how we know and what we know as readers become one through the mediation of the language of love. [. . .]

The key to the way Donne effects the revelation of love is lodged in the linguistic medium of the two lovers' symbiotic relationship, namely, "soules language" (22), which "tells" them what they love: "This Extasie doth unperplex / (We said) and tell us what we love" (29–30). Soul's language is common to both lovers because "good love" (23) has transformed their two souls into a single "abler soule" (43) possessing knowledge of its own essence: "Wee, then, who are this new soule, know, / Of what we are compos'd, and made" (45–46). In other words, the two lovers have become what they know, namely, a single abler soul formed out of an "interinani-mating" love (41–44), the essence of which is language.

The knowledge gained, however, carries with it the necessity to share that knowledge with "weake men" in its embodied form: "To our bodics turne wee then that so / Weake men on love reveal'd may looke" (69–70). The lovers' descent "T'affection, and to faculties, / Which sense may reach and apprehend" (66–67) does not state that it is their sense which is to apprehend their love; they have already acquired an understanding of what they love, derived, in part, from the "sense" conveyed to them initially by their bodies:

> We owe them thankes, because they thus,
> > Did us, to us, at first convay,
> Yielded their forces, sense, to us,
> > Nor are drosse to us, but allay. (52–55)

Their descent, like God's descent into the world, is necessary so that "weake men," for whom divine love requires a visible presence, "on love reveal'd may looke."

The form in which their love is to be revealed is the subject of the poem's closing lines: "Loves mysteries in soules doe grow, / But yet the body is his booke" (71–72). Here Donne's speakers seem to say that as *embodied* lovers they will preserve, with only "small change" (76), the linguistic nature of their relationship by serving as Love's text. In effect, their verbal ecstasy—"this dialogue of one"—is destined to become the visible text of a corresponding ecstasy, namely, "The Extasie" we have before us as Donne's poem. On one level, then, the poem appears to speak to the process of writing itself, that is, to the process of converting the intellection of love as a "dialogue of one" into "love reveal'd." The desired effect, we can assume, is a corresponding metaphysical structure of response.

Donne meets the challenge of revealing a love that coheres in "soules language" by means of three formal conditions basic to the dramatic monologue: a single speaker, a silent interlocutor, and a dramatic situation. Unlike the lyric, which is the expression of the individual speaker's state of mind, the dramatic monologue dramatizes the subtle "contact of minds" between the speaker and the silent interlocutor. Because the interlocutor does not voice his or her thoughts, the speakers words alone must bear the impress of the interlocutor as they impinge on the reader's consciousness, a condition of the dramatic monologue that clearly distinguishes it from the form of the lyric. [. . .]

Sympathy, however, is not to be understood as a purely neutral frame of mind. Rather, it is an intentional, or responsive, disposition that functions as an aspect of meaning. Langbaum briefly describes it as a "humanitarian attitude." "The Extasie" alludes to a similar state of mind:

> If any, so by love refin'd,
>   That he soules language understood,
> And by good love were growen all minde,
>   Within convenience distance stood,
>
> He (though he knew not which soule spake,
>   Because both meant, both spake the same)
> Might thence a new concoction take,
>   And part farre purer then he came. (21–28)

For the reader, as for the hypothetical witness and the two lovers, the condition of understanding a dialogue of one is to adopt a "convenient distance" from Love's text so as not to impose one's own desires and values on the life of the cognitive event. The reader is to "negotiate" meaning in the same way that the two lovers have arrived at their joint understanding of love. The implication is that meaning is neither the exclusive property of the text nor of the reader. Rather, it is coextensive with each.

—Helen B. Brooks, "'Soules Language': Reading Donne's 'The Extasie,'" *John Donne Journal* 7, no. 1 (January 1988): pp. 47–51.

Thematic Analysis of
"A Valediction Forbidding Mourning"

Izaak Walton, a contemporary of John Donne, suggested that "A Valediction Forbidding Mourning" has a strong autobiographical element, namely that it is addressed to Donne's wife, Anne More, on the occasion of his leaving for a continental trip in 1611. If this is true, then the poem owes its serious tone and message to the sense of foreboding Donne felt about leaving her. In fact, his intuition turned out to be correct, for she gave birth to a stillborn child while he was away.

Nevertheless, this interpretation is somewhat speculative. This poem is part of *Songs and Sonnets,* a volume whose general theme is the exploration of love's true nature. As David Novaar has said in his book *The Disinterred Muse* (citing yet another critic, A.J. Smith), the poems that comprise this volume all have a common theme: erotic life, in which a committed passion subsumes sexuality. Although the love poems which comprise *Songs and Sonnets* do not say exactly the same thing—in fact, their range is quite diverse, from satire and wit to serious meditation on the spiritual and philosophical nature of love—they do present a coherent perspective: sexual love is both an element of and a means to a lasting and transcendent relationship, one that goes far beyond the limits of the physical and sensuous. Donne's achievement in these poems is extraordinary for his time—the creation of a "rhetorical" space where the body and soul must be united in order to achieve lasting unity both in this world and the next.

To begin our discussion of this particular poem we should, once again, take the title of this poem as Donne's announcement of his intention. A valediction is the lover's farewell or leave-taking, in which he demonstrates his sensitivity to the woman he leaves behind; the title suggests that he will persuade her not to be sad while he is gone. That melancholia will be stated in the most extreme terms as he remonstrates with his lover not to lose all hope of his return, as if he had died. Thus, the title of the poem suggests that the poem's speaker is offering his beloved a form of consolation. He will be constructing an argument that will convince his beloved of the soundness of his advice, proving to her that he will indeed return to her, because true love can never be ruptured. The poem that follows the title is the evidence that the speaker hopes he will convince his beloved of this everlasting love, guaranteeing their inseparability.

In the first stanza, the poet draws an analogy between the lovers' relationship and the death of the righteous; he alludes here to the resurrection of both body and soul, affirming wholeness even in death: "As virtuous men pass mildly away, / And whisper to their souls to go." The strength of this argument is further buttressed in the next two lines, where Donne acknowledges and rejects all those who do not believe in the eternal integrity of the body and soul, thus responding to a possible invalidation of his argument: "Whilst some of their sad friends do say / The breath goes now, and some say, No." John Freccero's in "Donne's Valediction: Forbidding Mourning" (*English Literary History*, 30 (1963): 335–376) asserts that this poem not only precludes grief in the same way that the death of virtuous men forbids mourning, but that the comparison hints that "just as the righteous soul will at the Last Judgment return to its glorified body, so the voyager will return to his beloved" (p. 338).

Having thus established the integrity of the body and soul in death, Donne takes the argument a step further. This is a truly audacious step, for it advocates that the lovers unceremoniously take their leave of this world: "So let us melt, and make no noise." Here (as in "Love's Alchemy") we have a reference to alchemy, which sought to purify and refine base materials into pure and rarefied essences. Donne also once again rejects the courtly love tradition by banishing some of the commonplace rhetoric of that stylized and artificial love: "No tear-floods, nor sigh-tempests move; / 'Twere profanation of our joys / To tell the laity our love." Thus, the love relationship of this poem is a refined one, and although rooted in this world, it has at the same time a foothold in the celestial.

We see this in the third stanza when Donne places the lovers in a world beyond mortal fears such as earthquakes which, in his time, were thought to be portentous. "Moving of th' earth brings harms and fears, / Men reckon what is did and meant." Instead, the lovers will merely experience the tremors of the celestial realm: "But trepidation of the spheres, / Though greater far, is innocent." Once again, these lovers possess this exalted and privileged status because their love for each other is so spiritual and strong. They have forged an inseparable bond, unlike lovers of this world who are the victims of their own fear of death. "Dull sublunary lovers' love / (Whose soul is sense) cannot admit / Absence, because it doth remove / Those things which elemented it." The soul is contained here within parentheses, strengthening the argument that those who fear death are not whole, but instead are only marginally alive.

The next stanza repeats the alchemic metaphor of a refined love so spiritually composed that it cannot be defined through human language: "by a love so much refined / That our selves know not what it is." These lines contain strands of meaning twisted together. First, alchemists were thought to delve in highly esoteric knowledge, which could be understood only by a very select few; this specialized knowledge produced the need for a language that was not intelligible to the average person. Second, in writing the word "our selves" as two words, Donne again asserts his confidence that the lovers' physical separation cannot be cause for alarm, for their reunion is assured. "Our souls therefore, which are one, / Though I must go, endure not yet / A breach, but an expansion, / Like gold to airy thinness beat."

The next stanza presents one of the most famous examples of the metaphysical "conceit," that of the lovers being compared to a geometric compass. "If they be two, they are two so / As stiff twin compasses are two; / Thy soul, the fixed foot, makes no show / To move, but doth, if th' other do." The compass, an illustration of constancy in change, draws a complete circle—a symbol of perfection. Like the two legs of a compass, the lovers are both separate and inextricably bound to each other; thus they are assured of eventual reunion. "And though it in the center sit, / Yet when the other far doth roam, / It leans and hearkens after it, / And grows erect, as that comes home."

The poem ends with the speaker assuring his beloved that their faith in one another guarantees his return. "Thy firmness makes my circle just; / And makes me end where I begun." ❀

Thematic Analysis of
"The Canonization"

As in much of Donne's poetry, the very title suggests the multiple levels of compacted meaning that accrue to the central conceit: what it means to be canonized. The application of the descriptive term "canonical" simultaneously carries political, religious, personal, and literary themes with which Donne took issue.

If someone has been canonized, they have received the great honor of formal admission into the church calendar. In general terms, however, to be canonized is to be installed in an ecclesiastical office, with all the institutional powers that go along with such an exemplary position. More generally still, to be canonized means to conform with an established doctrine and adhere to its strictures. As a descriptive term "canonical" relates to the various hours of the day that the Church has designated for prayer and devotion (for instance, the Church even had said precisely the hours of the day when the marriage ceremony could be performed in a parish church in England). Finally, as Donne reworks the canonization conceit, the concept can be applied to institutions other than the church, a connotation that is not necessarily positive. All of the above definitions will become germane to our analysis of the poem.

The first stanza begins dramatically with a frustrated outburst. We are lead to believe that the undisclosed addressee is creating various obstacles and otherwise rankling the speaker's avowed intention to pursue love. "For God's sake hold your tongue, and let me love, / Or chide my palsy, or my gout"; in other words, find something more appropriate to complain about, such as the real problems which ail me. And if that does not provide ample material, then look to your own issues and focus on them. "Flout, / With wealth your state, your mind with arts improve." Obviously, the speaker has very little respect for his interlocutor, who is clearly consumed with getting and spending and the empty vanities of this world. Indeed, the speaker goes so far as to suggest that his addressee should turn his attention to the royal court; that suggestion bears a considerable jibe as it becomes a social commentary on the justice system and on the status of the kingship. "Observe His Honor, or His Grace, /Or the Kings real, or his stampèd face."

Donne highlights various types of fictions, both legal ("His Honor") and royal ("His Grace"). He condemns his addressee (and by extension many others as well) for being blinded to the fact that an aura has developed around certain political institutions, so that no one notices the fact that images of the king are as powerful as his actual presence. During the long history of kingship a powerful notion has been formed concerning the king's "political body," a body that no longer requires his actual physical attendance.

Further, because the speaker feels that this other person is interfering with his ability to pursue love, the complaint carries the suggestion that Donne is once again denouncing the courtly love tradition that was based on the lover being wholly absent from the lady. This sort of love existed in the imagination only, rather than in the body and soul. Thus, Donne will also be attempting to correct this centuries-old literary tradition that operated on a fixed set of "canonical" rules.

The second stanza is every bit as dramatic as the first. We can almost hear the deafening tirade as the speaker challenges the addressee to prove that an affirmation of his sexuality is injurious to anyone. "Alas, alas, who's injured by my love?" The focus here is on the courtly love tradition, and the poet seems to preempt the addressee from criticizing his treatment of love by anticipating the objections that conventional readers may have to his radical overturning of his predecessors. The poet recites many of the stock phrases and trappings of that artistry, asking "[w]hat merchant's ships have my sighs drowned? / Who says my tears have overflowed his ground?" He demonstrates that his affirmation of real passion is the proper subject of poetry, claiming that "the heats which my veins fill" do not "[a]dd one man to the plaguy bill." If we are still not convinced that his perspective is a true antidote to the fictions by which he is surrounded, the speaker compares himself to soldiers who must seek wars and lawyers who must find "litigious men" to justify their existence, whereas the speaker has achieved a lasting and constant relationship with his beloved. Amid all the empty noise and maneuverings, "she and I do love."

The next stanza continues the argument about the speaker's relationship with the beloved, stating that they do not have need for conventional epithets ("Call us what you will") as their love is true ("we are made such by love"). Even more significant, they are responsible for their own actions, which harm no one else. "We're tapers too, and at our cost die." Thus, several themes are being reiterated here, all of which refer back to the first two stanzas.

First, the commonplaces of courtly love cannot do justice to their relationship and, secondly, the courtly love tradition of unrequited love is exactly what is being corrected through the physical consummation of their relationship. This is indicated in the metaphor of the self-consuming candle, referring to an old superstition that held that intercourse shortens life. If we apply this same superstition to the courtly love tradition then, by extension, the consummation of love would mean the end of stories about unrequited and impossible love.

Second, Donne once again points out the injustice of other institutions that are destructive to society, namely the soldiers who seek war and the lawyers who seek quarrelsome clients, and thus do not at their "own cost die." Having established that the lovers harm no one else, Donne now takes their exemplary relationship to the level of absolute indestructibility by comparing it to an eagle (a symbol of strength), a dove (a symbol of mercy), and the legendary phoenix (a symbol of everlasting life). "The phoenix riddle hath more wit / By us: we two being one are it." In making an analogy between their love and these legendary symbols, Donne memorializes their lives, granting them honors bestowed on those who have been canonized.

Another implication is embedded within the legend of the phoenix, a sacrificial theme, for the phoenix was said to be consumed by its own flames every five hundred years, and then rise anew from its ashes. This theme brings an additional dimension to the "canonization" conceit, for it elevates the lovers' relationship to the level of the saints. The written account of a saint's life, known as a hagiography, always included the theme of extraordinary courage in the face of perilous threats and the sacrifice of the saint's own life. Thus, Donne implies that he is bestowing the highest and most spiritual institutional approval at the same time that he overturns a worn-out literary convention.

The fourth stanza expands upon the sacrificial theme of the lovers' sainthood, beginning with the noble declaration that their love will live on in the next world, even if they are to be denied in this one. Their relationship will become legendary. "We can die by it, if not live by love, / And if unfit for tombs and hearse / Our legend be, it will be fit for verse."

The compensatory gesture here suggests that the poet is not quite as self-assured of success as we have been led to believe up to this point. This uncertainty is contained within the phrase "if unfit for tombs." He gains consolation that even if not appreciated, his work is too radical to ever be ignored, and thus he will live on forever in his work. "And if no piece of chronicle we prove, / We'll build in sonnets pretty rooms." Furthermore, the poet declares that he will fashion a "well-wrought urn" that like the phoenix, will contain not only ashes but the promise of return. In that way his poems will become songs of prayer and praise that will lead to canonization. "And by these hymns [i.e., his poetry] all shall approve / Us canonized for love."

This analogy of his work to a hymn contains the idea that his contribution is on a level with the very beginnings of Christianity in the fourth century. This was a time especially marked by persecution and the martyrdom of the saints. The metaphor leads to the last stanza where the poet installs himself, in the most authoritative sense of the word, by declaring that he and his mistress have now become symbols of religious inspiration. "And thus invoke us: You whom reverend love / Made on another's hermitage." So audacious is Donne's pursuit of the canonization conceit, that he leaves us with the most memorable image of all: he and his mistress, now in heaven, are now beseeched to send down a pattern of ideal love for general distribution amongst the populace. "Countries, towns, courts; Beg from above / A pattern of your love!" Donne concludes triumphantly, having brought a new "religion" in which all people may participate, regardless of status or social class. ❀

Thematic Analysis of
"A Hymn to God the Father"

As a genre, in Donne's day the hymn was already two thousand years old. It was a religious form of poem used by the ancient Greeks to praise their gods. When the Christian church of St. Augustine appropriated it, its definition was restricted to praise sung to God. According to P.M. Oliver, Donne's contribution to this genre was to "divorce it from its eulogistic origins," which is to say that his main purpose was not to express approbation, but to engage God in a debate.

During the Renaissance, there was a degree of suspicion about hymns among the Protestants, especially Calvin, who opposed their use in congregational worship. Thus, we should not be surprised that Donne is reviving a form that was no longer fully sanctioned. An inherent tension was built into his use of hymn at a time when he and his countrymen believed that before creating the world, God had already chosen those who would be saved and those who would be condemned.

Keeping this background in mind, we can begin to analyze these tensions in "A Hymn to God the Father," one of Donne's *Divine Poems*. Whether this poem is autobiographical, and if so, to what degree, is uncertain. While Donne is characteristically fond of punning on his name in the last two lines of each of the three stanzas ("When thou hast done, thou hast not done"), the poem lacks any other specific information to support an autobiographical reading. In a far more subtle way, however, this poem can easily be read as Donne's questioning artistic achievement, expressing a genuine anxiety that he will be forgotten to posterity. To this end, each of the three stanzas contains a key word that indicates both the speaker's state of mind and the status of the argument being made.

In the first stanza, the speaker's tone is that of a supplicant, imploring God to forgive him for a sin which he has not committed but merely inherited by virtue of having been born. "Wilt thou forgive that sin where I begun, / Which is my sin, though it were done before?" Rather than accepting the teachings of the Protestant Church, Donne is expressing a feeling of a grave injustice having been done to him, an injustice he cannot escape no matter what direction he runs. "Wilt thou forgive that sin through which I run, And do run still, though still I do deplore." His use of the word *deplore* carries a great deal of emotion. *Deplorare*, the Latin root, meant to weep bitterly and lament one's fate. In Donne's day, the word also had come to mean a state of mind in which one has abandoned all hope. This being the case, it is quite clear that Donne is expressing a feeling of extreme helplessness when confronting the fearful prospect that he may not be one of the elect, and a powerlessness to change what has been preordained. Donne does not allow himself to remain powerless, however. Instead, he offers a counter-statement to this unjust condemnation, boldly declaring that his argument will invalidate this same divine injustice, enabling him to win the debate through superior rhetoric—the poem itself.

In the second stanza, the speaker assumes a far more combative and challenging stance, this time asking God to forgive him not only for having won the battle but also for influencing other rebellious spirits to feel equally empowered. An implicit rhetorical device is used here, known as prolepsis, whereby one party in a debate speaks of future events as if they had already taken place. The device presents a skillful opportunity to preempt an adversary's response before it is offered. Needless to say, it is also a demonstration of bravado, especially here in the speaker's prediction that the power of his word will prevail among the congregation. "Wilt thou forgive that sin by which I have won / Others to sin? And made my sin their door?" The sin being railed against is something the speaker initially attempted to shun, but he has nevertheless not only yielded to it, but engaged in it for years, indeed for a time well beyond his initial attempts at denial. "Wilt thou forgive that sin which I did shun / A year or two, but wallowed in a score?"

Donne's use of the word *score* unequivocally states his radical agenda. In its more general application a score is a marker, recording of something that has taken place, a line that indicates a boundary, and a tallying of points in a game with two or more opponents; all of this relates to Donne's prediction that he shall be the victor. While these definitions are all applicable, however, the word also carries other implications: it is a descriptive word used when one suddenly bursts into impetuous speech, as well as a figurative term for being beyond reason. Thus it is an apt description of Donne's feelings of having been wronged. Finally, a score refers to a footstep or imprint; this again underscores Donne's concern with being remembered for his artistic achievement.

The last and third stanza brings us squarely to this issue, specifically Donne's anxiety about the subversion of the Church of England within his poetry. "I have a sin of fear, that when I have spun / My last thread, I shall perish on the shore." Here he exchanges a general and indirect sin (i.e., the original sin in which all were considered tainted) for a very specific sin, fear about his poem. As part of his agenda of overturning Church doctrine, he has also woven the pagan into his poem with his implied reference to the Parcae of classical myth, the goddesses who spin the thread of human fate; he even hints at a reference to the Virgilian underworld where the souls who have not been buried cannot be ferried across the River Styx.

The final question is how to interpret the conclusion. "Swear by thy self, that at my death thy Son / Shall shine as he shines now and heretofore." Does "thy Son" refer to Christ? Or is it a pun on the word "sun?" If so, then Donne's poem is self-referential, consumed with his own need to be assured that what he has done will be recorded for all posterity. Both meanings may be valid, since Donne is surely anxious about his public declaration of unorthodox views that oppose the teachings of the Protestant Church. Indeed, both themes are present throughout the poem, and his plea for mercy and assurance will resolve the "sin of fear" he now substitutes for "the original sin" with which he never felt a connection. "And, having done that, thou hast done, / I fear no more." Perhaps, in the final analysis, the most he could hope for is a substitution of sins, because by invalidating tradition he must, of necessity, invoke new anxieties. ❀

Critical Views on
"A Valediction Forbidding Mourning,"
"The Canonization," and
"A Hymn to God the Father"

JAY DEAN DIVINE ON THE SYMBOLIC
IMPORTANCE OF THE COMPASS

[While most commentators have examined the circle which
the compass draws, in the excerpt below from his article
"Compass and Circle in Donne's 'A Valediction: Forbidden
Mourning,'" Jay Dean Divine discusses the symbolic importance of the compass itself.]

It is surprising to notice that of the many published essays and notes on
the compass figure in John Donne's "A Valediction: Forbidding Mourning"
almost all are in fact considerations of the significance of the circle
described by the compasses. W. A. Murray, for instance, has pointed out
the connection between the circle in Donne's conceit and the seventeenth-
century chemical symbol for gold—a circle with a point in the center. [. . .]

While critical focus on the symbolic importance of the circle in "A
Valediction: Forbidden Mourning" (and elsewhere in Donne) is merited,
that focus has preempted consideration of the compass itself, at least in
one central aspect which seems, in retrospect, obvious. Just as the visual
figure of the circle is integral to the unity of associations in the poem, so is
the visual figure of the compass. When paired the figures recreate visually
the A and W, Alpha and Omega, of the Greek alphabet, and recall immediately the wide use of "Alpha and Omega" in ecclesiastical literature as a
term signifying both "completeness" and the omnipotence of God. The
context most familiar to the modern reader is perhaps that of the King
James Bible: "I am Alpha and Omega, the beginning and the end, the first
and the last" (Rev. 22:13; see also Isa. 44:6).

The viability of the circle as a universal symbol of eternity, of God, of
the beginning and end of all created things, is of course enhanced by the
visual allusion to Alpha and Omega. But more to the point, the nexus of
the poem, the ennobling of human love by suggesting its spiritual dimensions, is similarly reinforced. This central motif is introduced in the second
stanza of the poem. The lines

> T'were prophanation of our joyes
> To tell the layetie our love
>
> [7–8]

imply the presence of the divine in the love of the speaker for his mistress. The divine essence is of course not present in "dull sublunary lovers love" (whose soul is sensual).

While the speaker's love is ennobled by its spiritual qualities, it is at the same time a very human love (note line 20, "Care *lesse* eyes, lips, and hands to misse," rather than "Care *not*"). For Donne—at times a Renaissance Neoplatonist and at times not—the functioning of both soul and body is necessary for completeness in love. Here the Alpha and the Omega serve not merely to reinforce, but to consummate the human, erotic aspects of the poem's theme. The Alpha is of course a male or phallic image and the Omega is female. Moreover, because literary convention has long recognized that both creation and destruction are implicit in sexual union, the "beginning and end" association is again evoked, this time within a different thematic context. Donne is suggesting that while the soul of his ideal love is spiritual, it becomes complete only with the acceptance of the physical. Scholars have been increasingly critical of that view which sees Donne as a reformed rake; we now realize that although he well knew that physical passions are an inescapable part of human love, he knew also that only through human love could he arrive at divine love. Human love is thus exalted and purified.

—Jay Dean Divine, "Compass and Circle in Donne's 'A Valediction: Forbidden Mourning,'" *Papers on Language and Literature* 9, no. 1 (Winter 1973): pp. 78–80.

A. B. CHAMBERS ON GLORIFIED BODIES AND THE "VALEDICTION"

[In the excerpt below from his article "Glorified Bodies and the 'Valediction: Forbidding Mourning,'" Professor A. B. Chambers discusses the argument of the poem in terms of the two types of materials on which it depends, namely "glorified bodies" in their perfected form on Judgment Day and the materials of alchemy which sought a purification of base metals into a "glorified and golden state."]

The imagistic structure and much of what might be called the "argument" of Donne's famous "Valediction" depend heavily on two bodies of material which appear to be, at least at first glance, totally unrelated to one another. The first is the theology of glorified bodies, of bodies as they are to be in perfected form when resurrected on Judgment Day. It now seems strange that such a theology could even exist since there is and necessarily can be no experiential basis for it, but this fact did not trouble earlier religious writers at all. Many of them, including Donne himself, were confident that they knew, and knew rather precisely, what to expect at their own resurrection. The second body of material, now less esoteric to many readers than it once was, is alchemy. However unrelated or even antithetcal to scholastic theology alchemical literature appears to be, there is in fact considerable duplication in imagistic usage because of the fact that works of alchemical theory regularly refer to the metaphorical "death" of a metal and to its "resurrection" in a glorified and golden state. A number of symbols appear in both systems of thought; gold, thinness, airiness, circles and/or spheres, the sun, and symbolic arithmetic are among them. the parallelism at times becomes so close that it would be impossible to tell whether alchemy or theology is being talked about if a given passage were to be read without some context as a guide. Some writers, moreover, are quite deliberately talking about both subjects simultaneously. Since this conflation of subjects was intentionally made in earlier times, I have found it impossible to separate out the two contributory parts. In what follows, I cite the evidence for glorified bodies, whether human or metallic or both, as the case demands.

Donne's poem, to begin with, while not a "divine" poem [recalls] specifically the eleventh article of the Creed: "I believe . . . in the resurrection of the dead." It is in discussion of that belief that one finds why virtuous men can and *should* pass mildly away and what they anticipate themselves to be in the ultimate future. The first term of Donne's initial simile—

> As virtuous men passe mildly away,
>   And whisper to their soules, to goe,
> Whilst some of their sad friends doe say,
>   The breath goes now, and some say, no

—quite clearly presents a standard contrast of the kind that divines, as well as poets, liked to make. John Baker, expounding the Creed, writes that

> they that are wel perswaded in minde of the resurrection of their bodies, can not but at the last houre of death depart ioyfully & merrily out of this life. . . . But they that are not fully perswaded of this true article die very vnwillingly, & with griefe & sorrowe of minde.

Ben Jonson, in a two-line epigram "Of Death," arrives at a similar conclusion:

> HE that feares deathe, or mournes it, in the iust,
> Shewes of the resurrection little trust.

It is, of course, precisely a confident trust in the resurrection and in the reunion of body and soul then to occur which allows virtuous men to pass

mildly away, and it is, implicitly at least, a mistrust of that event which produces mournful friends more concerned with literal "breath" than with—
Donne's pun is obvious—*anima*, the soul as well as the breath. The initial
contrast, then, is between proper and improper ways of viewing death,
ways which in turn are dependent on belief or disbelief in the resurrection.

This first stanza therefore relates not only to the poem's title, "farewell,"
but also to the second term of the initial simile:

> So let us melt, and make no noise,
> > No teare-floods, nor sigh-tempests move,
> T'were prophanation of our joyes
> > To tell the layetie our love.

"Layetie" and its implicit contrast—the "priests" or possibly, as in "The
Canonization," the "saints" of love—combine with "prophanation.
[Considering the context] of "melt," "floods," and "tempests," the con-
text of alchemy also becomes important. [. . .]

These "operations" include a "killing" of the metal by reducing it to its
constituent parts and restoring it to life in a reconstructed but more perfect form. The alchemical process, whether for human or metals, begins
with "dissolution," which some, according to Flammel, call "*Death* . . . and
from hence are proceeded so many *Allegories* of *dead men, tombes*, and
sepulchres." Others, he continues, "have called it . . . *Mollification* . . . *Liq-
uefication* . . . because that the *Confections* are melted." At this point,
unhappily for the practicing alchemist, the parallels temporarily ended. It
was always possible to "flood" or ruin an experiment and thereby cause a
"tempest" or, as Donne has it in the "Nocturnal," a "chaos." In God's
alchemy, however, resurrection is assured.

> —A. B. Chambers, "Glorified Bodies and the 'Valediction: Forbidding
> Mourning,'" from *John Donne Journal* 2, no. 6 (June 1982): pp. 1–3.

JOHN FRECCERO ON THE CIRCLE OF LOVE

[John Freccero is the author of *Dante: A Collection of Critical
Essays* (1965). In the excerpt below from his article "Donne's
'Valediction: Forbidding Mourning,'" Freccero discusses
Donne's efforts to unite the body with the soul, which he
describes as a "rescue," and focuses on the circle of perfection
drawn by the compass as the poet's way of humanizing love.]

Among English poets who underwent the influence of Italian love poetry of the Renaissance, John Donne stands out as one who sought to reconcile the errant soul to its body once more. This meant rescuing human love from both the angelic mysticism and the erotic formalism of the Italian tradition and restoring it to its proper domain: humanity. Donne was primarily concerned neither with the angel nor with the beast, but rather with the battlefield separating them, long since vacated by the Italians; insofar as he defended that middle ground in the question of human love, his poetry marked a return to a more "medieval" sensibility. It is the thesis of this paper that his most famous image, that of the compass in "A Valediction: Forbidding Mourning," protests, precisely in the name of incarnation, against the neo-Petrarchan and neoplatonic dehumanization of love. It makes substantially the same point made by Love to the young Dante three hundred years before: angelic love is a perfect circle, while beasts move directly and insatiably to the center; *tu autem non sic.*

Human love is neither because it is both; it pulsates between the eternal perfection of circularity and the linear extension of space and time. The compass which Donne uses to symbolize it, therefore, traces not merely a circle but a dynamic process, the "swerving serpentine" of Donne's poetry and of his thought. This is the essence of the love celebrated in the "Valediction: Forbidding Mourning," a vertical reconciliation of body and soul. At the end of its gyre, on the summit where time and eternity meet, stands the lovers' Truth: "hee that will / Reach her, about must, and about must goe . . ." (Satyre III, 80–1). Because Love's truth is incarnate, however, its celestial apex is at the same time the profound center of an interior cosmos which is governed by its own laws and bounded by the lovers' embrace. For such lovers there can be no breach between the macrocosm of space and time and the microcosm of Love because all of reality is circumscribed by the point upon which their love is centered. With its whirling motion, Love's compass describes the expansion of the lovers' spirit from eternity to time and back again.

This motion is the archetypal pattern of Love's universe, the principle of coherence joining matter and spirit throughout all levels of reality. By itself, however, this principle is purely formal. The image of the compass cannot convey the vital reality which underlies it and gives to the poem its symbolic substance.

In his sermons, Donne expresses the incarnate dynamism of humanity with the figure of married love: "As farre as man is immortall, he is a married man still, still in posession of a soule, and a body too." "Death," he tells us, "is the Divorce of body and soule; Resurrection is the Re-union. . . ." It is from this exegetical commonplace that the argument of the "Valediction: Forbidding Mourning" derives its force. If incarnation is not simply an abstraction, but rather the informing principle of reality, then the terms of the analogy are reversible and the union of body and soul may serve as a figure for the love of husband and wife. Donne the preacher wrote of death and resurrection in figurative terms of the separation and reunion of husband and wife; as a lover, in the poem we are about to discuss, he had written to his beloved of their separation and eventual reunion in figurative terms of death and resurrection: "As virtuous men passe mildly away . . . So let us melt. . . ." The poem reversed a traditional figure and gave to the neo-Petrarchan dialectic of presence and absence a new metaphysical meaning. As the soul is indissolubly linked to the body, so the husband is linked to his faithful wife. The "Valediction" is a *congé d'amour* which precludes grief in the same way that the death of virtuous man *forbids mourning;* that is, the simile with which the poem begins glosses the poem's title by hinting that, just as the righteous soul will at the Last Judgement return to its glorified body, so the voyager will return to his beloved.

—John Freccero, "Donne's 'Valediction: Forbidding Mourning'" from *English Literary History* 30, no. 3 (March 1963): pp. 336–38.

ALLEN TATE ON MOVEMENT IN THE "VALEDICTION"

[Allen Tate is a well-known critic and poet. His critical works include *Forlorn Demon Didactice* and *Critical Essays* (1953) and, among the collected editions of his poetry, *Collected Poems 1919–1976* (1977). In the excerpt below from his book *Essays of Four Decades,* Tate discusses the idea of movement in "Valediction: Forbidding Mourning" where the moment of death marks the passage of lovers to a higher from of love, and which movement is accomplished by the Aristotelian circle uniting physical with divine love.]

> As virtuous men pass mildly away
>> And whisper to their souls, to goe,
> Whilst some of their sad friends do say,
>> The breath goes now, and some say no:
>
> So let us melt and make no noise,
>> No teare-floods nor sigh tempests move;
> 'Twere prophanation of our joyes
>> To tell the layetie our love.

I believe that none of Donne's commentators has tried to follow up the implications of the analogy: the moment of death is like the secret communion of lovers. The first thing that we see is that lovers die *out of* something *into* something else. They die in order to live. This is the particular virtue, the Christian entelechy or final cause of mankind, and the actualization of what it is to be human.

The logical argument of "A Valediction: Forbidding Mourning" is a Christian commonplace. Through the higher love lovers achieve a unity of being which physical love, the analogue of the divine, not only preserves but both intensifies and enlarges. The implicit symbol of this union is the Aristotelian circle of archetypal motion. Union is imagined first as a mathematical point where physical and spiritual union are the same; then as an expanding circle of which the point is the center. The analogy is complete when the two legs of the draftsman's compasses become congruent in the lovers' embrace, so that the legs form a vertical line standing on the "same" point. Thus Donne "reduces" a Platonic abstraction to actual form by contracting the circumference, "absence," to the point, "reunion," on the human scale, of the lovers.

Logically the mathematical point precedes the circle of which it is the center; literally it also has priority, since the lover begins his journey from the point. But the poem as action, as trope, asserts the priority of the circle, for without it nothing in the poem would move: the lovers in order to be united, or reunited, have got first to be "separated," the woman at the center, the man at the enlarging circumference, even though the separation is further and larger union. The visual image of the expanding circle is the malleable gold, which by becoming materially thinner under the hammer expands indefinitely, but not into infinity; for this joint soul of the lovers is a "formulable essence" which abhors infinity. The material gold disappears as it becomes absolutely thin, and is replaced by pure, anagogical "light"— another Christian commonplace that needs no explanation. Donne fills his circle with a physical substance that can be touched and seen; but it is the particular substance which archetypically reflects the light of heaven. Yet all this light which is contained by the circle is only an expanded point of the gold, they always occupy the same "space," and are never separated. Space is here the "letter" of a nondimensional anagoge; and likewise the circle widening towards infinity. Thus spatial essences are the analogical rhetoric of a suprarational intuition.

But "A Valediction: Forbidding Mourning" is a poem, not a philosophical discourse. And since a poem is a movement of a certain kind in which its logical definition is only a participant, we have got to try to see this poem, like any other, as an action more or less complete. For an action, even of the simplest outline, in life or in art, is not what we can say about it; it rather is what prompts us to speak. The Christian commonplaces that

I have pointed out are not Donne's poem; they are, as letter and allegory, material factors that it is the business of the poet to bring to full actualization in rhetoric, the full linguistic body of the poem which ultimately resists our analysis, is the action, the trope, the "turning" from ignorance to knowledge, from sight to insight. This tropological motion is the final cause of the poem, that toward which it moves, on account of which its logical definition, its formulable essence, exists. And it is the business of criticism to examine this motion, not the formulable essence as such.

Donne's two opening stanzas announce the theme of indissoluble spiritual union in an analogy to what seems at first glance its opposite: dissolution of soul from body. First we have dying men (not one man, not trope but allegory) who "whisper to their souls, to goe'" then, in the second stanza, lovers who "melt *and* [my italics] make no noise." The moment of death is a *separation* which virtuous men welcome, and the lovers are about to *separate* in quiet joy ("no teare-floods nor sigh-tempests move"). For the lovers too are "virtuous"—infused with a certain power or potency to be realized. They have no more fear from separation from each other than dying men from death, or separation from life. If the lovers foresee no loss, they may expect a gain similar to that of the dying men.

—Allen Tate, *Essays of Four Decades* (Chicago: Swallow Press, 1968): pp. 247–49.

MAUREEN SABINE ON THE AUTOBIOGRAPHICAL ASPECTS OF "THE CANONIZATION"

[Maureen Sabine has written the introduction to *The Femall Glory, 1635* by Anthony Stafford (1988). In the excerpt below from her article "No Marriage in Heaven: John Donne, Anne Donne, and the Kingdom Come," Sabine discusses the autobiographical aspects of "The Canonization" and reads the poem within the context of the religious and cultural conditions which influenced the poet. In that same article, Sabine then contrasts the healing aspects of young love in "The Anniversarie" in contrast to "The Canonization."]

If, as Bald believes, "The Canonization" alludes to the early years of Donne's marriage to Anne, when they had nothing much to live on or for except sex, then the speaker's wild claims for lovemaking appear a noble attempt by the poet to look beyond his marital miseries and hold fast to "the kingdom, the power, and the glory" that is revealed to men and women in their bodies. St. Paul had assured the Romans that "God has imprisoned all human beings in their own disobedience only to show mercy to them all" (11:32). The chief mercy that God shows to the rebellious lovers of "The Canonization"—and perhaps to Donne himself after his own release from prison—is the sexuality where they can offer their "bodies as a living sacrifice, dedicated and acceptable to God" (Rom. 12.1). When Donne wrote "The Canonization," the "living sacrifice" that constituted the heart of the Eucharistic service was provoking passionate debate, dissent, and recusancy among Catholics and Anglicans. The worship that Christians could safely conduct in private, without need of a priest, the communion that remained freely available to all despite "difference of sex" or creed was the lovemaking, the living sacrifice of highly sexed bodies, that is given both sacrilegious and sacramental importance in "The Canonization." The speaker of this poem has at once the worst opinion and the highest regard for sexual love. His "palsie," "gout," and "five gray haires" (ll. 2–3) are symptoms of an unrepentant fornicator; for frequent intercourse was commonly regarded as a *petit mort* that led to premature aging, baldness, and death. Yet these same infirmities and the aroused sexual state that they presume are given startling new meaning by Christ's assurance that: "every hair on your head has been counted" and is precious in the sight of a God of love (Luke 12.7). Likewise, as has been often noted, the speaker and his mistress give a sensational new angle to Christ's death on the Cross and Mary Magdalene's witness to his Resurrection from the tomb when they "dye and rise the same, and prove / Mysterious by this love." Their sexual climax is an idolatrous parody of Christ's deliverance of man from sin but also exults in the revolutionary vision that the sexual consummation of a love match like Anne and John's helps to complete the work of redemption, the work of redeeming men and women not from, but in the flesh. The poet's own plea for mercy to his estranged patron, the Lord Keeper Sir Thomas Egerton, "that redemption was no less worke than creation," is similar in spirit to "The Canonization" and suggests how he tried to do in art, what he failed to do in life, which was to defend and glorify "the remarkable error" of his marriage and the sexual abandon that was regarded as such undignified behavior. To Egerton and the other keepers of Elizabethan law, a lover's presumption that there is a divine meaning to his sexual misadventure would have seemed the height of arrogance and absurdity. Yet it is hard not to cry mercy for that frail, fool-hearty, but brave hope that Donne formulated in "The Canonization" and perhaps composed in the social exile of Mitcham.

> You whom reverend love
> Made one anothers hermitage;
> You, to whom love was peace, that now is rage,

> Who did the whole worlds soule extract, and drove
> 　　Into the glasses of your eyes
> 　　So made such mirrors, and such spies,
> That they did all to you epitomize,
> 　　Countries, Townes, Courts: Beg from above
> 　　A patterne of your love!

(ll. 37–45)

The hope is that if the Body of Christ was breaking up as an institutional power and a sacramental force in the world, indeed if marriage was no longer a sacrament, the *corpus mysticum* survived, concealed in lovers' bedrooms, sexed bodies, and amorous sonnets. The lovers themselves are held up in place of the sacred host, which was once elevated. It is they who provide "Countries, Townes, Courts" with that eye-glass, or round, mirrored window, that opens like the Eucharistic monstrance of old on the mystery of Christ died, risen, and come again. But what a momentous change Donne has wrought in this poem. For the pornographer's visual images—the hole and the prick, the unspeakable sexual acts and aids—have become "something else," something sacred and mysterious. In this moment of revelation, Christianity seems to implode as it is driven in on itself and forced to see its own unedifying history through lovers' eyes. [...]

In "The Anniversarie," it is not perfect love but young love that casteth out fear. Couples who meet and fall in love in youth must be pardoned if they naively imagine themselves to be immortal. Even the weary, pained speaker of "The Canonization," who should know better, feels a godlike flame flickering in the passionate love of later life, the love that gathers intensity from the melancholy presentiment of death. But the speaker of "The Anniversarie" has not yet been battered about the heart and glories in the fact that he has loved one whole year and not just "one whole day" ("Womans constance," l. 1). Like the young Paul McCartney singing "When I'm sixty-four," he cannot really imagine getting old nor can he imagine that his longstanding relationship will be subject to time or their love subject to temporal authority. He has a lot to learn and he learns fast.

> All Kings, and all their favorites,
> 　　All glory'd of honors, beauties, wits,
> The Sun it selfe, which makes times, as they passe,
> Is elder by a yeare, now, then it was
> When thou and I first one another saw:
> 　　All other things, to their destruction draw,
> 　　　　Only our love hath no decay;
> This, no to morrow hath, nor yesterday,
> Running it never runs from us away,
> But truly keepes his first, last, everlasting day.

(ll. 1–10)

By the second stanza, the speaker has become wise to the fact that their love is mortal and because mortal, corruptible. In "A Valediction of my name" Donne's speaker would pursue a similar line of reasoning. But it will generate a different and more malignant fear: that his mistress might be corrupted by lust and so deal a mortal blow to the enduring spirit of their union. The speaker of "The Anniversarie" contemplates mortality more philosophically, but only because he deadens the pain of love and softens the unbearable truth with which he opens the second stanza. "Two graves must hide thine and my coarse, / If one might, death were no divorce" (ll. 11–12). The stronger the attachment, the more grievous will be the sorrow of separation. Death does us part. Some critics have maintained that "The Anniversarie" can have no bearing on Donne's marriage to Anne but must be alluding either to their premarital relationship or another love affair because the couple in the poem occupy two different graves. But I think they miss the point that is being tacitly reiterated—that "true deaths, true marriages untie" ("Womans constancy," l. 8). Whether their union is officially recognized or not, long or short-term, this couple enjoy a "true maryage" because they have dramatically touched, altered, and interanimated each other's lives. Yet, however much this love has shaped their very souls, they have come together, as Augustine put it, through a "corruptible and mortal conjugal connection" that will be dissolved by death and corruption in the grave. God surrenders what he has joined.

Donne's speaker promises his mistress more than the sun and the moon. He promises her a love that "hath no decay" (l. 7), that will make life eternal. He then gently disabuses her of these high hopes and shows her the two graves, which are brutal proof of the fact that death is a divorce, however much either the poet himself or his critics or any of us might wish otherwise. As John Carey has shown, Donne had great difficulty in accepting the orthodox Christian belief that the soul could endure separation from the body at death, could enjoy heavenly life in the interim without this body, or suffer the long wait until the physical resurrection. For Donne conceived of the relationship of the soul and the body in terms of the marital union. "God married the Body and Soule in the Creation," he preached and "as farre as man is immortall, man is a married man still, still in possession of a soule, and a body too; and man is for ever immortall in both. . . . For, though they be separated. . . . they are not divorced" (*Sermons* 7, 257). . . . Yet one of the reasons, I propose, why the thought of death and resurrection steals like a thief in the night into his love poems is because he was haunted by Christ's admonition to his disciples: "in the resurrection they neither marry, nor are given in marriage, but are as the angels of God in heaven" (Matt. 22. 30). The death of the body was therefore the death of love in human form and flesh, which is the only love we know. [. . .]

Therefore, the speaker's closing declaration in the second stanza, "when bodies to their graves, soules from their graves remove" (l. 20), has sombre implications, though it is unclear from the third and final stanza of the poem whether the speaker is anticipating an existence in heaven before or after the physical resurrection.

—Maureen Sabine, "No Marriage in Heaven: John Donne, Anne Donne, and the Kingdom Come," in *John Donne's "desire of more,"* ed. M. Thomas Hester (London: Associated University Presses, Inc, 1996): pp. 235–39.

Dayton Haskin on Biographical Interpretation

[In the excerpt below from his article "On Trying to Make the Record Speak More about Donne's Poems," Dayton Haskin discusses "The Canonization" in terms of the history of its criticism and argues for a biographical interpretation, especially in light of the fact that 17th-century readers would have read the poem as Donne's justification for his marriage.]

One "extraordinary result" of Brooks's having made of "The Canonization" a paradigmatic poem for the New Criticism is that antithetical critics treat it as if it has always been considered a literary monument. Through most of the three centuries after Donne wrote it, however, the poem received little attention. That it should have taken so long for "The Canonization" to be thought significant in literary history might be regarded either as something of a curiosity or as further evidence for the doctrine that meanings are constructed, not merely found. Nonetheless, attention to the history of reading "The Canonization" through the long period between its first appearance in print in 1633 and the publication of "The Language of Paradox" in 1942 suggests that the marginal status of a poem now thought to be quintessential Donne may not have been so much an accident as it was an "extraordinary result" of another confrontation with Donne's poem by an earlier and powerfully influential reader. In large measure the history of "The Canonization" was shaped by the writer who sought to canonize Donne's life, his first biographer, Izaak Walton. Without ever explicitly mentioning the poem, Walton's *Life and Death of Dr. Donne* long served as a severe restraint on interpretation of "The Canonization" until, at the end of the nineteenth century, that same *Life* was suddenly seen to provide grounds for interpreting the poem in ways almost diametrically opposed to those in which it had previously been read.

Besides the fact that "The Canonization" enjoyed no particular prominence before the 1940s, a second striking feature about the history of interpreting the poem is that it took more than two and a half centuries until anyone seems to have proposed reading it in relation to details known about the marriage. Walton's *Life*, a book that through the eighteenth and nineteenth centuries enjoyed much wider popularity than Donne's Poems, had claimed that writing poetry had been for Donne a youthful diversion and that "most" of his poems, which had been "loosely scattered" in manuscripts, were written before he was twenty. Yet Walton had also given great scope to the story of Donne's secret wedding, when he was nearly thirty, and its disastrous aftermath. By the nineteenth century various retellings of the story were appearing regularly in literary handbooks and popular literature. As interest in the poetry revived, several other lyrics by Donne, including "The Relique," which is related to "The Canonization" by virtue of their sharing sources of imagery in medieval hagiography, were said to reflect incidents in this relationship with Anne More. It was not until the end of the century, however, that anyone proposed in print that "The Canonization" had been written as the poet's defense of their marriage.

This essay seeks to trace the history of reading "The Canonization" before the publication of "The Language of Paradox" and to account for the fact that the poem was only belatedly fitted into what might have seemed an obvious biographical context, a context from which Brooks's interpretation asked readers again to prescind. It is not my purpose to urge any particular date of composition for "The Canonization" and "The Relique," nor to defend the proposition that they were written in Donne's maturity. It is plausible that they were among the poems to which Ben Jonson was referring when he said that Donne had "written all his best pieces err he was 25 years old." There are good reasons for reading "The Canonization" in the context of Renaissance poems that promise immortality; and the poem may be thought to involve an elaborate and derisive hoax perpetrated on just those vulgar readers in the future who, in what "The Relique" refers to as "mis-devotion," overlook the outrageousness of the conceit whereby the lovers are "canonized" for Christ-like sexual exploits. To trace the slow emergence of an explicitly biographical interpretation of the poem one need not accept the proposition that Donne *wrote* the poem as an attempt to justify his marriage, but one needs to take seriously the likelihood that the poem was *read* that way by some seventeenth-century readers.

—Dayton Haskin, "On Trying to Make the Record Speak More about Donne's Poems," in *John Donne's "desire of more,"* Ed. M. Thomas Hester (London: Associated University Presses, Inc, 1996), pp. 39–41.

[Cleanth Brooks is a well-known and highly respected literary critic. His critical works include *William Faulkner: Toward Yoknapatawpha and Beyond* (1978). In the excerpt below from his book *The Well-Wrought Urn: Studies in the Structure of Poetry,* Brooks discusses the central paradox in "The Canonization," and the conflicting meanings which result from Donne's treatment of profane love as if it were divine.]

I have said that even the apparently simple and straightforward poet is forced into paradoxes by the nature of his instrument. Seeing this, we should not be surprised to find poets who consciously employ it to gain a compression and precision otherwise unobtainable. Such a method, like any other, carries with it its own perils. But the dangers are not overpowering; the poem is not predetermined to a shallow and glittering sophistry. The method is an extension of the normal language of poetry, not a perversion of it.

I should like to refer the reader to a concrete case. Donne's "Canonization" ought to provide a sufficiently extreme instance. The basic metaphor which underlies the poem (and which is reflected in the title) involves a sort of paradox. For the poet daringly treats profane love as if it were divine love. The canonization is not that of a pair of holy anchorites who have renounced the world and flesh. The hermitage of each is the other's body; but they do renounce the world, and so their title to sainthood is cunningly argued. The poem then is a parody of Christian sainthood; but it is an intensely serious parody of a sort that modern man, habituated as he is to an easy yes or no, can hardly understand. He refuses to accept the paradox as a serious rhetorical device; and since he is able to accept it only as a cheap trick, he is forced into this dilemma. Either: Donne does not take love seriously; here he is merely sharpening his wit as a sort of mechanical exercise. Or: Donne does not take sainthood seriously; here he is merely indulging in a cynical and bawdy parody.

Neither account is true; a reading of the poem will show that Donne takes both love and religion seriously; it will show, further, that the paradox is here his inevitable instrument. But to see this plainly will require a closer reading than most of us give to poetry.

The poem opens dramatically on a note of exasperation. The "you" whom the speaker addresses is not identified. We can imagine that it is a person, perhaps a friend, who is objecting to the speaker's love affair. At any rate, the person represents the practical world which regards love as a silly affectation. To use the metaphor on which the poem is built, the friend represents the secular world which the lovers have renounced.

Donne begins to suggest this metaphor in the first stanza by the contemptuous alternatives which he suggests to the friend:

> *. . . chide my palsie, or my gout,*
> *My five gray haires, or ruin'd fortune flout. . . .*

The implications are: (1) All right, consider my love as an infirmity, as a disease, if you will, but confine yourself to my other infirmities, my palsy, my approaching old age, my ruined fortune. You stand a better chance of curing those; in chiding me for this one, you are simply wasting your time as well as mine. (2) Why don't you pay attention to your own welfare—go on and get wealth and honor for yourself. What should you care if I do give these up in pursuing my love. [. . .]

There is one more factor in developing and sustaining the final effect. The poem is an instance of the doctrine which it asserts; it is both the assertion and the realization of the assertion. The poet has actually before our eyes built within the song the "pretty room" with which he says the lovers can be content. The poem itself is the well-wrought urn which can hold the lovers' ashes and which will not suffer in comparison with the prince's "half-acre tomb."

And how necessary are the paradoxes? Donne might have said directly, "Love in a cottage is enough." "The Canonization" contains this admirable thesis, but it contains a great deal more. He might have been as forthright as a later lyricist who wrote, "We'll build a sweet little nest, / Somewhere out in the West, / And let the rest of the world go by." He might even have imitated that more metaphysical lyric, which maintains, "You're the cream in my coffee." "The Canonization" touches on all these observations, but it goes beyond them, not merely in dignity, but in precision.

I submit that the only way by which the poet could say what "The Canonization" says is by paradox. More direct methods may be tempting, but all of them enfeeble and distort what is to be said. This statement may seem the less surprising when we reflect on how many of the important things which the poet has to say have to be said by means of paradox: most of the language of lovers is such—"The Canonization" is a good example; so is most of the language of religion—"He who would save his life, must lose it"; "The last shall be first." Indeed, almost any insight important enough to warrant a great poem apparently has to be stated in such terms. Deprived of the character of paradox with its twin concomitants of irony and wonder, the matter of Donne's poem unravels into "facts," biological, sociological, and economic. [. . .]

For us today, Donne's imagination seems obsessed with the problem of unity; the sense in which the lovers become one—the sense in which the soul is united with God. Frequently, as we have seen, one type of union becomes a metaphor for the other. It may not be too far-fetched to see both as instances of, and metaphors for, the union which the creative imagination itself effects. For that fusion is not logical; it apparently violates science and common sense; it welds together the discordant and the contradictory.

—Cleanth Brooks, *The Well-Wrought Urn: Studies in the Structure of Poetry* (New York: Harcourt Brace Jovanovich, 1947): pp. 10–12, 17–18.

Joseph E. Duncan on Donne's Concept of Resurrection

[Joseph E. Duncan is the author of *Milton's Earthly Paradise: A Historical Study* (1972). In the excerpt below from his article "Resurrections in Donne's 'A Hymne to God the Father' and 'Hymn to God my God, in my sicknesse'" Duncan discusses the first poem in terms of three types of resurrection which refer back to the poet's spiritual experience during the time of its composition.]

Between 1620 and 1630 John Donne preached eleven sermons on the resurrection, building on a threefold interpretation of resurrection in five of these sermons, including three Easter sermons. In this threefold interpretation the first conception is that of a resurrection from persecution or calamities, for a society or for an individual. The second conception is that of a resurrection from sin through grace in this life. The third conception is that of the resurrection to glory, the resurrection of the saved with a transfigured body, to dwell eternally in heaven. Donne emphasized that all three conceptions were rooted in the resurrection of Christ.

Examined in the light of Donne's sermons on resurrection, his "A Hymne to God the Father" and "Hymne to God my God, in my sicknesse," while making no clear reference to a resurrection from persecution or calamities, dramatize the second and third conceptions. They reveal an assurance of the resurrection of the soul from sin in this life and accept this spiritual resurrection as an "infallible seale" (as Donne calls it in one sermon) of the resurrection of the body to glory. Donne's sermons on the resurrection provide an illuminating context for the spiritual experience of the speaker in these two hymns. Apparently written during Donne's grave illness in late 1623, both poems may be read as his poetic interpretation of his spiritual experience. They reveal successive aspects of the speaker's spiritual experience, but with the reverse of the order in which the poems are usually printed.

The conception of the spiritual resurrection from sin was derived from various passages in the New Testament, especially from the resurrection referred to in Revelations 20:6: "Blessed and holy is he that hath part in the first resurrection: on such the second death hath no power, but they shall be priests of God and of Christ, and shall reign with him a thousand years." Although many early Christian commentators interpreted the "first resurrection" literally as the actual reign of Christ on earth with the glorified martyrs for a thousand years, Donne along with many Protestant writers followed Saint Augustine and the Geneva Bible in interpreting it as a spiritual resurrection in this life. In rejecting the literal interpretation, Saint Augustine objected to the "immoderate carnal banquets" and other material luxuries envisioned by the chiliasts or millenarians. The marginal commentary in the Geneva Bible explains that the "first resurrection" is "to receive Jesus Christ in true faith, and to rise from sinne in newenes of life." Donne was thoroughly familiar with the Geneva Bible; he used it throughout his *Essays in Divinity* and quoted from it frequently in his sermons. [. . .]

This assurance of the spiritual resurrection and the joy in the certainty of the physical resurrection appear to be at the heart of the spiritual experience in Donne's "A Hymne to God the Father" and "Hymne to God my God, in my sicknesse." These two poems are closely related and reflect successive stages in the pattern of spiritual experience discussed repeatedly in the sermons. "A Hymne to God the Father" shows the joy in the spiritual resurrection as an "infallible seale" of the resurrection to glory.

Though some critics have emphasized the sense of sin, fear, and irresolution in "A Hymne to God the Father," this poem, while it shows Donne's awareness of sin, is marked by his confidence that his sins are forgiven. These are sins which Donne has confessed and continues to confess and which God has forgiven and continues to forgive. In confessing his sins frankly and fully, "more" and "more," Donne expresses a repentance that is vital to the spiritual resurrection. In his poem "To Mr. Tilman after he had taken orders" (1619–20). Donne implies that he too, after taking orders, has experienced spiritual regeneration, felt "new feather'd with coelestiall love" (l. 22). Moreover, Donne's *Devotion upon Emergent Occasions,* written at about the same time as "A Hymne to God the Father," expresses a similar pattern of sin and forgiveness. Addressing God, Donne sees his rising from his sickbed as "by thy grace, and earnest" of a "*resurrection* from *sinne*" and to "*everlasting glory.*" Donne speaks of "*those sinnes,* which I have truely repented and thou has *fully pardoned*" but he knows that he has to depend on "*to morrowes* grace too."

One of the closest parallels to the spiritual experience described in "A Hymne to God the Father" occurs in one of Donne's sermons of 1624. One passage is a public statement of the steps in sin and spiritual resurrection that are expressed privately in the hymn; in fact, it could serve as Donne's commentary on his hymn. In this sermon Donne speaks of sinning as "a sinking, a falling" ever lower, "from Originall into Actuall, in Habituall sins," but then proceeds to the great theme of the sermon: "sin is death, and that needs a resurrection." Through the spiritual resurrection God raises one from the "death past," "present death," and "future death" of sin. The same pattern appears in the "Hymne to God the Father." As Donne confesses and God forgives one kind of sin after another, he is raised from spiritual death. The hymn is structured to lead through the confession of sins to the assurance of the resurrection from sin and the consequent resurrection to glory. Donne goes on to confess "more" sins after he feels those just related have been forgiven. The pattern of the poem leads from the forgiveness of original sin ("that sinne where I begunne"), of actual sin ("by which I wonne others to sinne"), of habitual sin (that he has "wallowed in, a score") and, finally, to the forgiveness of his "sinne of fear" that he will perish.

—Joseph E. Duncan, "Resurrections in Donne's 'A Hymne to God the Father' and 'Hymne to God my God, in my sicknesse,'" *John Donne Journal* 7, no. 2 (May 1988): 183–86.

DAVID J. LEIGH, S.J., ON DONNE'S RELATIONSHIP WITH HIS WIFE

[In his article, "Donne's 'A Hymne to God the Father': New Dimensions," David J. Leigh's reading of the poem emphasizes the autobiographical context, focusing on Donne's wife, Anne More. With reference to that relationship, he explores the paradox of human and divine love.]

In the flood of commentaries on Donne since the 1950's, none of the devotees of what Eliot called the lemon-squeezer school of criticism has pressed much new meaning from "A Hymne of God the Father." In fact, no one has adequately explained why it was perhaps Donne's favorite poem, the only one he had set to music and sung at St. Paul's. At the risk of ingenuity, I am suggesting that the final line of each stanza ("I have more") contains a highly significant play upon his wife's maiden name. This play on words not only adds a fuller dimension to the line itself but also enriches the poem as a final expression of Donne's fascination with the paradox of divine and human love.

There is little reason to be surprised at any play on words in Donne, even on his own name. In the famous letter to his wife, Anne More Donne, after losing his preferment because of their clandestine marriage, Donne signed himself, "John Donne, Anne Donne, Un-done." And the 1623 "Hymne" itself hinges on the line (sometimes printed with his name spelled out): "When thou hast done, thou hast not done." The same poem also contains one of his most often repeated puns—sun /Son—in "at my death thy Sunne / Shall shine as it shines now." Potter and Simpson, in their introduction to *The Sermons of John Donne,* discuss Donne's fondness for puns in his sermons, both his own and those of the Latin Fathers of the Church. They list the play on sun/Son as the most frequent pun in his sermons. [...]

We must assume, of course, that Anne More was the most important person in Donne's personal life. The decision to marry her cost him his career at court and led to his gradual movement toward the ministry, eventually to the deanship of St. Paul's. But the transition, as Walton, Gosse, and modern biographers tell us, was extremely painful. [...]

If this relationship with Anne More was at the heart of Donne's personal life, the paradoxical relationship of human to divine love is at the heart of his poetic vision. Even a brief survey of his sermons and earlier poetry provides a background for a new reading of his "A Hymne to God the Father." In theological terms we can say that Donne used an interplay of the two mystical traditions—the *via affirmativa,* which emphasized the similarity and continuity of the human and divine spheres; and the *via negativa,* which stressed the ultimate discrepancy between the two levels. But beyond both "ways" was Donne's occasional portrait of the final transcendence in the paradoxes of heavenly union in which the human and the divine, the nothing and the All, are resolved. [...]

In his marriage sermons, which are often too pedantic for modern tastes, Donne occasionally rises to rhetorical heights of wit. In his sermon for the marriage of Robert Sandys and Margaret Washington on May 30, 1621, Donne provides a small treatise on the triple analogy between secular married love, Christ's love for the soul and the Church, and divine love for people in heaven. However traditional, this underlying analogy is a clear example of the affirmative vision of human love as analogous to and fulfilled in divine love. [...]

This brief résumé of Donne's quite traditional use of the paradoxes of married and divine love provides an apt prelude to what I suggest is a more complete reading of "A Hymne to God the Father." The usual interpretation of the first stanza, for instance, treats the last two lines ("When thou hast done, thou hast not done, / For, I have more.") as referring merely to "more" sins than just original sin ("that sinne where I begunne") and repeated personal sins ("those sinnes through which I runne"). The allusion to the original sin of Adam and Eve might suggest that the "more" involved a certain imperfection in Donne's relationship with his wife. Not that he would fully subscribe to Milton's later version of Adam's fall as an excessive attachment to Eve. But the final "I have more" might imply at least some inordinacy in Donne's love for his wife, an inordinacy that must be purged before God can "have Donne" completely. In any case, the last line of the stanza, if taken as referring to Anne More, can mean this: insofar as the marriage of Donne and More made them one, God cannot be done until He has saved them both together.

The problem of Donne's attachment to his wife may, however, involve the possibility of some further guilt. Several biographers have suggested that Donne felt responsible for burdening his young wife with marriage and children so early that he eventually precipitated her death. However anachronistic this suggestion may sound, it is not impossible that Donne felt some remorse at causing her a life of poverty and obscurity for so many years. Another possible sin he may have experienced was that of despair and bitterness over her death—natural enough but a sign of weakness he may have felt in need of purging.

In all of these shadings, we find variations on the fundamental theme of the *via negativa*—an excessive attachment to a creature that must be moderated before one can be prepared for union with god the Father. This interpretation adds a further dimension to the second stanza, in which Donne asks forgiveness for leading others into sin ("made my sinne their doore") and for some habitual sin ("wallowed in, a score"). Here, if the final "more" refers to his wife, Donne may be asking further forgiveness for his failure to provide the "mutual help" which he preached in his marriage sermons to be the chief responsibility of spouses. There is also the remote possibility, if the biographers are correct in ascribing some close relationship (perhaps to Mrs. Herbert) to Donne's life after Anne's death in 1617, that he is here asking pardon for such "infidelities."

All of these potential interpretations become more likely when we reread the final stanza. For there Donne expresses an inexplicable "sinne of fear" that he will "perish on the shore" of heaven, just before attaining the presence of the Father. If Donne's fear includes a distrust of the imperfections in his relationship with his wife, then his fear is less than rational.

And such a fear can be appropriately overcome by God swearing by His own "self" (three in one just as Donne and More are two in one) that his "Sunne" will continue shining on Donne. For, according to Donne the preacher, it is in the risen Son of God that Donne entered marriage, a relationship which is sign of Christ's love (Eph. 5). This marriage "in the Lord" is also the affirmative way by which Donne was led through human to divine love, and is a temporal union foreshadowing the eternal heavenly union. Thus Donne has completed the negative way and "has no more"; now he can leap to the transcendent union where by not having anything he will have All.

—David J. Leigh, S.J., "Donne's 'A Hymne to God the Father': New Dimensions," *Studies in Philology* 75, (1978): pp. 84–86, 90–92.

Overview of the Holy Sonnets

Donne's religious poetry is collectively known as the Divine Poems. These were first published in the second postumous edition of his poetry (1635). The largest group of Divine Poems are the 19 Holy Sonnets. In them, Donne relies on the existing poetic tradition of the sonnet, which he uses as a vehicle for the exposition of his own religious struggles, expressing the tension between his avowed religion of Calvinism and the strong Catholic upbringing of his childhood.

Donne was not the first to use the sonnet for spiritual debates, and among his forbears were two notable Elizabethan poets: Thomas Vaux (1509–56), whose speaker boldly insists on being heard, most specifically about his dissipated past, in the poem entitled "Of the Instability of Youth" ("O Lord, forget these faults and follies all!") and William Hunnis, who in his collection of poems, *A Handful of Honeysuckles* (1583), addresses God in the audacious manner which we encounter in Donne's speakers ("O Jesu, if thou do withdraw / Thy comfort for a time, / Let not despair take hold on me, / For any sinful crime"). Nonetheless, despite these literary groundbreakers, critics acknowledge that Donne's contributions to the "holy" sonnet were unique. These contributions include a dramatic presentation of a specific theological point of view in each of the poems, creating a "space" for Donne to rehearse different religious views and philosophical perspectives, often in the form of a debate, as well as a bold and daring imagery that frames such questions as the immortality of the soul and the assurance of heavenly rewards for mortal trials and tribulations.

An essential part of Donne's Catholic upbringing was the teaching that the performance of good works in his lifetime, demonstrating a faithful adherence to the teachings of the Church as well as contrition for any transgression of those precepts, would assure the soul's future happiness in the afterlife. Indeed, the medieval allegory, as previously mentioned in the biography, mandated a reading strategy that included the anagogical level dealing with the eternal life of the soul after it had transcended the captivity of mortal existence. This type of reasoning is referred to as an eschatology. It concerns itself with the four last things: death, judgment, heaven and hell.

Catholicism's simple equation (i.e., a good mortal life equals a happy eternity) was erased by Protestant theology. Instead, Calvinism taught that some souls are "elected" for salvation before birth and thus are predestined to receive God's grace in heaven. Furthermore, and most distressingly, no "good works" or other acts of faith could be perform to change this "fixed" status. This radical difference from the Catholicism of Donne's earlier training was a source of tremendous anxiety for the poet, as well as many others. Despite the loss of a "way to salvation," they were required to follow a strict moral code according to the orthodox teachings of Calvinism.

In his book, *Donne's Religious Writings*, P. M. Oliver compares the *Holy Sonnets* with the *Songs and Sonnets* and sees a similar intention on the poet's part. "The parallel with the amatory verse illuminates Donne's use of the *Holy Sonnets* to experiment with what it would be like to be a mortalist, or to feel almost certainly damned . . . —above all, the way Donne utilises them to explore the position of a believer passionately concerned about matters of salvation and damnation in the first place." ❀

Thematic Analysis of "Death Be Not Proud"

"Death Be Not Proud," number X of the *Holy Sonnets* that was published in various editions between 1635 and 1669, begins as a radical undermining of death's power. It vigorously attempts to deny death any hope for its continued existence.

The poem begins with a personification, a rhetorical device that attributes human qualities to an abstract concept, here death, and addresses it as an already-defeated opponent. Assigning of human attributes to death is both the basis of Donne's enervating its power and the means by which he makes it accessible to mortal intervention and human vulnerability. "Death be not proud, though some have called thee / Mighty and dreadful, for thou art not so."

Here death is accused of the mortal sin of pride, one of the seven deadly sins of the Catholic Church and a sin adamantly proscribed by the Protestant sects as well. In order to render death vulnerable to human failings, Donne presents death as suffering from self-delusion about its own authority; it merely "imagines" that it has supreme power. "For those whom thou think'st thou dost overthrow / Die not, poor death, nor yet canst thou kill me."

Donne's next strategy is to expose death's power as existing only in strong images. In fact, however, those images merely represent rest and sleep, and therefore they are nothing to be feared. "From rest and sleep, which but thy pictures be, / Much pleasure; then from thee much more must flow." These images are so pleasant, the poet argues, that the implication must be that death is something to be sought after, as desirable as sleep at the end of a busy day. "And soonest our best men with thee go, /

Rest of their bones, and soul's delivery." When Donne diminishes death to a mere sleep, he also may be expressing his wish to stop death in its tracks.

Donne seeks to completely reverse death's sway over the most exalted of men, including the king and all who occupy a position of power: "Thou art slave to fate, chance, kings, and desperate men, / And dost with poison, war, and sickness dwell." He continues by pointing out death's enslavement by the very machinery through which it exerts its sovereignty, showing death's methods to be nothing more than trickery ("And poppy or charms can make us sleep as well").

Having pointed out to death all the pitfalls of its faulty thinking, Donne ends triumphantly. His absolute declaration of salvation affirms the immortality of the soul. "Why swell'st thou then? / One short sleep past, we wake eternally, / And death shall be nor more; death, thou shalt die." Thus, death is dealt the same unredeemed fate by which it previously exercised its absolute power over humanity. ❀

Thematic Analysis of "Batter My Heart"

"Batter My Heart," number XIV of the *Holy Sonnets*, begins with violent imagery: "Batter my heart, three-personed God; for You / As yet but knock, breathe, shine, and seek to mend." It presents the radiance of divine love in contrast to the trials and tribulations of the everyday world, trials that obscure and otherwise misdirect us from heavenly guidance.

Many of the clues to unlocking some of the subtle tensions within the poem are contained in the dominant metaphor, "to batter." In its most obvious definition, to batter an object or a person is to strike that object with repeated blows. It even contains a military context in which to batter is to break down walls or other obstructions in one's way. Within the context of this poem we come to understand that the speaker is frustrated by some obstacle that stands in the way of his connection to God. Perhaps the most interesting implication of the metaphor is the word's archaeological application, in which "to batter" means "to construct something on a slope or inclination."

With this context we arrive at Donne's underlying premise, namely, to allow God to remold and recreate him in a way that will lead him back to God. Furthermore, tools and implements are necessary to that process of reshaping, and yet God is the one who must take action; the poem's speaker remains passive. In the Christian metaphor of making all things new, grace is received, not achieved,

This is not a cozy and comfortable grace, however; the speaker does not simply want to be bolstered and supported by God, but instead he demands that God exert a severe and deliberately destructive action that will remold him according to divine will. "O'erthrow me, and bend / Your force, to break, blow, burn and make me new."

The next few lines of the poem explain the speaker's spiritual crisis in terms of a tortured emotional response. "I, like a usurped town, to another due, / Labor to admit You, but Oh, to no end!" The speaker feels like a "usurped town," and the images carries with it the undeniable sense of violation. He has been forcibly intruded upon and illegally seized, and the image alludes to a sexual connotation that is evident a little further on in the poem.

"Yet dearly I love You, and would be loved fain, / But am betrothed unto Your enemy." Thus, the speaker is experiencing a faltering faith, a psychic state poetically rendered in terms of a military battle, an inner feeling of divisiveness that is borne out in the marriage conceit that concludes this poem, containing in it the sexual implications mentioned earlier. "Except you enthrall me, never shall be free, / Nor ever chaste, except You ravish me." This is no pious, weak-kneed grace; instead, it is earthy, violent, and overwhelming. ✾

Critical Views on
"Death Be Not Proud" and
"Batter My Heart"

WILBUR SANDERS ON DONNE'S ATTEMPT
TO FAMILIARIZE MYSTERY

[Wilbur Sanders is the author of *Shakespeare's Magnanimity: Four Tragic Heroes, Their Friends and Families* (1978). In the excerpt below from his book *John Donne's Poetry,* Sanders discusses "Death Be Not Proud" as a "domesticated unknown," an attempt to familiarize, through bold imagery and verbal assault, that which must remain a mystery.]

Donne, of course, in both the erotic and the religious context, insists on the mysteriousness: the insisting is one of the marks that wonder is absent. But the last thing he means by love's mysteriousness (in 'The Canonization') is 'wavering motions sent he knows not whence'; when he tells us (in 'The Extasie') that 'Loves mysteries in soules doe grow', he immediately indicates the work of reference in which we can inform ourselves about the mystery ('But yet the body is his book'); and when, in 'Holy Sonnet 12', we are enjoined to 'wonder at a greater wonder' (the first wonder having proved rather a damp squib), Donne is at pains to explain exactly what this wonder is, thus effectively preventing our feeling anything more for it than a mild, straying curiosity.

It is a matter, finally, of the attitude you take to what you do not and cannot know. If you want it brought under immediate control, you can call it a mystery, and thus belittle it, tame it. It belongs thereafter to a category of things about which you know the precise extent of your ignorance. No further exertion can be expected of you: it is a mystery. Many of the *Divine Poems* offer us that domesticated unknown—a world in which even the unknown of death can be parcelled up and dispatched:

> Death be not proud, though some have called thee
> Mighty and dreadfull, for, thou are not soe.

No doubt the audacity is deliberate. But is the bland superficiality, as well? It's like nothing so much as the voice of Mr. Worldly Wiseman: 'I would advise thee, then, that thou with all speed get thyself rid of thy burden; for thou wilt never be settled in thy mind till then.' These poems may be divine, but they strike me as radically irreligious.

But we are not statutorily confined to the triumphal brassiness of 'Death be not proud'; there are other things, like the deep sonorities of that moving meditation upon death 'A Nocturnall upon S. Lucies day'. There, another impulse, not unlike Lawrence's and Wordsworth's, is at work; an impulse to abandon 'control' in the limited sense and search for some deeper ground of union with that which—however we struggle—still lies beyond us, vastness ultimately uncolonisable.

Once the comparison is made, the sonnet, impressive in its own battering way, sinks into proper perspective. You could say that the difference between the two poems is that, for the 'Nocturnall', someone has actually died whereas, for the sonnet, no one has and no one seems likely to. One is a poem about a death; the other a poem about Death whose author, in a manner thoroughly characteristic of 'mystery', seems to think that Death is somehow more important than dying and can be discussed without reference to it. But that's still to shallow a view of the case. The 'Nocturnall' is about more than a death. Momentous though the woman's death is, so momentous that only a quintessence of nothingness survives her, there is something even more momentous to which the catastrophe points—though 'points' is exactly the *wrong* word for the way we are made aware of it. [. . .]

When Donne attempts the same kind of persuasiveness, one is very conscious of rhetorical strain. He is trying to coerce, not celebrating in public language the unquestionable and the assured. So he relies upon a kind of verbal assault and battery which doesn't so much share the language with the reader, as use it as a weapon for the reader's subduing. And one is very conscious, too, of figure. Dunbar can hardly be said to personify at all; he talks about the objective 'dragon blak' and the visible 'yettis of hell'. Donne's personification of death is a blatant device, aimed at cutting death down to size, and the crisp cross-talk of quip and witticism indicates how well he knows he can't really get away with it.

> Death be not proud, though some have called thee
> Mighty and dreadfull, for, thou art not soe,
> For, those, whom thou think'st, thou dost overthrow,
> Die not, poore death, nor yet canst thou kill mee.
> From rest and sleepe, which but thy pictures bee,
> Much pleasure, then from thee, much more must flow,
> And soonest our best men with thee doe goe,
> Rest of their bones, and soules deliverie.

There for a moment Donne touches real conviction, a position from which he can contemplate death harmoniously both as a delivery of the imprisoned soul and a birth into life—but conviction most unlike Dunbar's in its subtle awareness of the double aspect of things.

A blustering sophistry supervenes:

99

Thou art slave to Fate, Chance, kings, and desperate men,
And dost with poyson, warre, and sicknesse dwell,
And poppie, or charmes can make us sleepe as well,
And better then thy stroake; why swell'st thou then?
One short sleepe past, wee wake eternally,
And death shall be no more; death, thou shalt die.

It may of course have been Donne's *intention* to carry off the whole affair with a kind of swaggering bravura, as a demonstration of his own freedom from rank superstition and craven fear. If so, it's an intention about whose realisation it's hard to get very excited. To deliberately confound the doctrine of the soul's immortality with the unconsolingly tautological sense in which Death is 'dead' for the individual once he has died, as if that were some kind of answer to the fear of death—it simply indicates how superficially that fear is present in the poem in the first place. It is paraded like a captive slave and publicly routed, but it is never met on the level where it really presses.

—Wilbur Sanders, *John Donne's Poetry* (Cambridge: Cambridge University Press, 1971): pp. 114–15, 126–27.

FREDERIC B. TROMLY ON SELF-DESTRUCTION IN "DEATH BE NOT PROUD"

[In the excerpt below from his article, "Milton Responds to Donne: 'On Time' and 'Death Be Not Proud,'" Frederic B. Tromly discusses "Death Be Not Proud" as a poem self-destructive to the speaker who desperately attempts to deny death.]

One of the most curious reticences in Milton's writing is the absence of any reference to the greatest English poet among his immediate predecessors, John Donne. Stranger yet, scholars have not been able to discover manifest borrowings from Donne in Milton's verse, and thus the assertion which Sir Walter Raleigh made sixty years ago remains undisputed: "As for the great Dean of St. Paul's, there is no evidence that Milton was touched by him, or, for that matter, that he had read any of his poems." There is, however, at least one significant like between the poets which has been overlooked: Milton's verses "On Time" indicate that he read and was "touched" by Donne's "Death Be Not Proud." [. . .] Both poems are highly rhetorical, declamatory credos which invoke then proceed to confute a personified metaphysical antagonist. Moreover, the structure of each poem is articulated in three parallel sections. First, each begins with a similarly cadenced command ("Death be not proud" and "Fly envious *Time*") which challenges the antagonist and associates and associates it with one of the seven deadly sins. Second, the body of each poem demonstrates (though in quite different terms) the impotence and self-destructiveness of the antagonist. And, finally, both poems conclude with a swelling apostrophe which powerfully asserts the triumph of mankind over the antagonist.

The two poems draw closest together in their concluding lines. Indeed, the penultimate lines of the poems are virtually isomorphic:

> One short sleepe past,   wee wake eternally
> [Donne]

> Attir'd with Stars,   we shall for ever sit,
> [Milton] [. . .]

Despite their similarities of phrase and theme, the two poems are radically different in tone and movement. "Death Be Not Proud" is notable (even among Donne's poems) for its brittle, shifting tone. After his triumph opening assertion of victory over Death, the speaker's certainty falters, and he proceeds to engage in casuistical and contradictory arguments with Death. Thus, he claims unconvincingly that Death must be more pleasant than rest and sleep because they are merely "pictures" of Death (lines 5–6), but then he suddenly shifts to argue that Death is a despicable slave who dwells "with poyson, warre, and sicknesse" (line 11). And after making the dubious argument that "poppie, or charmes can make us sleep as well" as Death (line 11), he immediately discounts the relevance of sleep by remarking that "One short sleepe past, we wake eternally" (line 13). The witty paradox ("death, thou shalt die") which concludes the poem is a final non sequitur, since the poet has not revealed why death's power is finite and ultimately self-destructive. The speaker has attempted to make a statement of faith similar to St. Paul's denial of death's sting (1 Cor. 15:51–58), but he lacks the requisite stability of belief to make a coherent declaration. The speaker ends where he begins; as a commentator has noted, "Had he been able to live by faith alone, he would have written no more than six lines: 1-4 and 13-14." His inability to maintain his lofty superiority to Death, suggests that the speaker himself may be one of the "desperate men" to whom he alludes. Ironically, what has been revealed to be self-destructive in the poem is not Death but rather the speaker's desperate attempt to argue against a fear that presses increasingly upon his mind and fractures his composure. [. . .] It seems safe to conjecture that Milton read Donne's poem not long after its publication, found its chop-logic and ambivalence disconcerting, and responded with a poem which attempts to make good its dubious triumph over mortality. If this be so, then "On Time" tacitly criticizes and rewrites "Death Be Not Proud."

—Frederic B. Tromly, "Milton Responds to Donne: 'On Time' and 'Death Be Not Proud'," *Modern Philology* (May 1983): 391–93.

PAUL M. OLIVER ON CALVINIST DOCTRINES IN "BATTER MY HEART"

[In the excerpt below from his book *Donne's Religious Writing: A Discourse of Feigned Devotion,* Paul M. Oliver discusses "Batter My Heart" as a poem presenting a critical perspective on Calvinist doctrines of grace and salvation.]

The note of almost unmixed joy (or, in Calvinist parlance, assurance of salvation) which one detects in 'This is my play's last scene' is struck nowhere else in the *Holy Sonnets.* It is tempting to suggest that its rarity is due to the comparative difficulty of creating drama out of experiencing what Perkins calls 'the inward peace of God' (Perkins 1597a, p. 151). The tendency of the other *Holy Sonnets* is towards the more critical perspective on Calvinist doctrines which is reflected in 'What if this present'. Donne ensures variety by concentrating on different aspects of Calvinism—and by adopting varying degrees of scepticism towards them. 'Batter my heart' (D, pp. 177–8), for example, alludes to the doctrine of the irresistibility of grace, and with less ambivalence than the final lines of 'Good Friday, 1613'. The speaker of the sonnet wants this grace to infringe his liberty, to do violence to him in order to make him belong to God. Stachiewski has observed that his opening words almost echo Perkins's description of the process of justification: 'he that will believe in Christ must be annihilated, that is, he must be bruised and battered to a flat nothing' (Perkins 1597b, p. 140). Knowing how far he is from the ideal, Donne's speaker feels that God's actions have proved pathetically inadequate as attempts to change him:

> you
> As yet but knock, breathe, shine, and seek to mend.
> (ll. 1–2)

What is needed is a massive show of strength:

> That I may rise, and stand, o'erthrow me, and bend

Your force to break, blow, burn, and make me new.

(ll. 3–4)

The Christian metaphor of 'making new' seems to be inserted in order to clarify that it is religious renewal that is sought—otherwise the reader could be forgiven for being perplexed by the degree of violence that is called for.

The sestet voices something stronger and harder to bear than disappointment. It now emerges that the speaker feels actually unloved:

Yet dearly'I love you, and would be loved fain,
But am betrothed unto your enemy . . .

(ll. 9–10)

'Your', rather than 'my' or even 'our', enemy makes it appear more irrational of God to allow this state of affairs to continue: God can't claim not to know the extent of the forces which the speaker senses pitted against him. Worse, he feels ensnared in an intimate relationship with the enemy. In Donne's time a formal betrothal taking the form of spoken promises to marry had legal status and, if followed by consummation, was as fully binding as marriage. Canceling a betrothal to the Devil will therefore be a more troublesome business than calling off a modern engagement. Hence the speaker's request to God to 'divorce' him. He wishes to be involved in a closer relationship with God, though not (this time) a relationship sanctioned by law and custom:

Take me to you, imprison me, for I,
Except you enthral me, never shall be free,
Nor ever chaste, except you ravish me.

(ll. 12–14)

This extraordinary image which sees chastity as something which can be gained as well as lost—and gained specifically through rape—is an indication of how unable the speaker feels to contribute anything of his own to the process of salvation. It constitutes a formal statement of his intention to do nothing; earlier in the poem he confessed to God that

I, like an usurped town, to another due,
Labour to admit you, but oh, to no end . . .

(ll. 5–6)

Since his own efforts have proved completely futile, he now intends to adopt a passivity of the most extreme kind. Divine rape seems to him to be the sole means of gaining the freedom from Satan he craves.

The belief that the individual is utterly impotent and saved solely as a result of all-powerful divine grace is straightforwardly Calvinistic, and the speaker's attitude is not marked by any noticeable scepticism towards it. However, as we saw when discussing 'Good Friday, 1613', the impulse to ask for irresistible grace is *not* orthodox. The elect are the recipients of it; those who are not elect cannot receive it, and no amount of begging on their part can alter this. In requesting it, the speaker parallels the mark-seeking speaker of 'What if this present' in his wish to be reassured of his election—except that a degree of self-examination to establish whether one was justified was sanctioned, whereas asking for irresistible grace was not. It would hardly be stretching things to see this request as another expression of the desire, entirely futile from the Calvinist point of view, to be removed from the ranks of the damned and to be counted among the elect. However one reads it, 'Batter my heart' (like 'This is my play's last scene' and possibly 'Good Friday, 1613') contains a brusque demand for something which Calvinists believed was entirely at the divine discretion.

—Paul M. Oliver, Donne's *Religious Writing: A Discourse of Feigned Devotion* (London and New York: Addison Wesley Longman, 1986): pp. 122–24.

William Kerrigan on "Batter My Heart"

[William Kerrigan is the author of *The Idea of Renaissance* (1989). In the excerpt below from his article "The Fearful Accommodations of John Donne," Kerrigan begins with a discussion of Donne's strategy of delicately balancing wit within the *Holy Sonnets* and focuses on "Batter My Heart" in terms of anthropomorphism, here defined as the "sexuality of God." He explains the disturbing rage of the last line as implying the ancient theological conceit of the soul's marriage to God.]

Poems such as "Batter my heart" and "Show me deare Christ" may appear desperately inventive, the work of a histrionic convert who "has to stimulate his awareness of God by dwelling on the awfulness of God." Like other Renaissance poets whose devotional verse has been assailed,

Donne has been defended by scholars assuming (however implicitly) that negative evaluations are directed, whether by ignorance or design, against the religion itself. Louis Martz and Helen Gardner, locating a tradition of formal meditation intended to achieve sensual immediacy, interior drama, and intense emotion, have disarmed objections by subtly disarming the poems, revealing those idiosyncratic, "tasteless" moments in the religious verse as the respectable, if passionate, consequences of devout contemplation. Still, many readers—all those, in fact, who find in the tastelessness of Donne either the sure measure of his limitation or the problematic force of his greatness—will sympathize with the hesitations of Frank Kermode, who writes of "Show me deare Christ": "Perhaps we dislike this metaphor (*Christ as mari complaisant*) because the image of the Church as the Bride is no longer absolutely commonplace; but having accepted the image we are still unwilling to accept its development, even though we see that the main point is the *glorious* difference of this from a merely human marriage. Something is asked of us we can no longer easily give. Many of the Holy Sonnets have this perilous balance; their wit is always likely to seem indelicate as well as passionate." [. . .]

For what disturbs Kermode, and what has disturbed critics of "Batter my heart," is Donne's eagerness to display the most anthropomorphic consequences of anthropomorphism—in short, to imagine with suspect the anthropomorphic vehicle. Perhaps the Ignatian exercises, with their extraordinary reliance on the power of corporeal images, promoted unsettling formulations of this kind. But these impressive poems appropriately raise the larger question of how and why Donne thought of man while thinking of God.

The problem of anthropomorphism was made acute for Christianity by the key doctrine of the inspired Scriptures. One sacred book held to contain all truth, every word used with full awareness of its connection to every other word—the tradition of Christian theology is, from this perspective, literary criticism of immense complexity, offering its own solutions to issues that have engaged the expositors of our own, relatively unseasoned discipline. Much of this literary speculation centered upon the intractably anthropomorphic character of the Bible and confronted, in this context, the relationship between the real and the fictive. One history of Christian theology might be plotted as the tension between limiting scriptural anthropomorphism as strictly as possible and licensing worshipers to pursue these inspired metaphors with full imaginative commitment. Excluding the simple anthropomorphism of various medieval sects, this history will be concerned largely with degrees of emphasis. Even Aquinas granted that God must be predicated with "life" and "personality," since it would be harrowing to suppose that the emotions invested in God, such as trust and love, were being presented to an impersonal force. [...]

Joan Webber has shown that Donne, in common with other Renaissance theologians, understood the verses of the Bible as "enfolding" significance. In preaching manuals the word "opening" referred to the division and interpretation of the text; the preacher merely exposed or dilated meanings assumed to be already present, though compressed, in the Bible itself. A sacred metaphor, like a seed bearing a tree, contained the full extension for its tenor. Perhaps this conception may help to describe that special way with conceits which we designate "metaphysical wit," indicating how Jack Donne became Dr. Donne without changing his habits of mind. [...]

Similarly, the disturbing rape in the last line of "Batter my heart" should be understood as implicit in the ancient theological conceit of the righteous soul's marriage to God. If the good man weds God, then the sinful man weds God's "enemie," and if God would claim this recalcitrant soul, then he must grant divorce and possess her by force. Given Donne's conception of sacred metaphor, the accommodated marriage would enfold infidelity, divorce, and even imprisonment. It would compress all the things which attend earthly marriages, the only ones we know and the only ones our language can properly signify. More specifically, it may be appropriate to mention, but absurd to continue mentioning, that Donne was in fact imprisoned by the father of his bride and that this poem resembles, with interesting shifts of identity and reattibutions of virtue, the drama of his own marriage:

> Batter my heart, three person'd God; for, you
> As yet but knocke, breathe, shine, and seeke to mend;
> That I may rise, and stand, o'erthrow me, 'and bend
> Your force, to breake, blowe, burn and make me new.
> I, like an usurpt towne, t'another due,
> Labour to'admit you, but Oh, to no end,
> Reason your viceroy in mee, mee should defend,
> But is captiv'd and proves weake or untrue,
> Yet dearly'I love you, and would be loved faine,
> But am betroth'd unto your enemie,
> Divorce mee, 'untie, or breake that knot againe,
> Take mee to you, imprison mee, for I
> Except you'enthrall mee, never shall be free,
> Nor ever chast, except you ravish mee.

To be sure, the poem is not so daring as it might have been. The phrase "three person'd God," for example, identifies the male lover addressed in Trinitarian terms, themselves derived by accommodation from the earthly family. I suppose that John Donne, in a certain mood, might have considered naming the holy lover as the "father" of this hapless bride and played out the grotesque results in allusions to incest—but Donne, thankfully, was not Crashaw. Nevertheless, "Batter my heart" does suggest by implication the details of its final phrase.

Though often described as a poem with three conceits of equal importance developed in successive quatrains, really the poem evolves from and toward a single metaphor. For the bride addressing her lover, equated to the soul addressing God, is the implicit situation throughout—unless we are to believe that suddenly and ridiculously, with the phrase "Yet dearely'I love you," our speaker changes sex. Revealed with increasing clarity from l. 9 to l. 14, the figurative terms of this address are assumed in the 'heart' of the opening line and continue to be assumed in the formal simile of the second quatrain. Thus the actual tenor of "Batter my heart" and "like an usurpt towne" is not, as in the usual reading, an experience of conversion. These subsidiary conceits have primary reference to the love of the soul, and during most of the poem the true sense of this crucial primary reference is left unsettled.

So clear as vehicle and so loose as tenor, the language of the first two tropes is purposefully dislocated. This speaker would have her heart reformed by the tinker's tools. But what exactly is she inviting from "three person'd God" when the terms of tinkering are translated to the terms of love? It will not suffice to recall the emblem tradition, where muscular arms wielding various tools reached from the clouds to batter or burn the miraculously suspended heart of the Christian Everyman, for the heart of this poem belongs to a misguided bride: the "emblem," if such it is, must be reshaped within the figures of another and controlling "emblem." The simile of the "usurpt towne" would appear to be clearer, at least in its reference to the interior betrayal of "weake or untrue" reason, since these words provide a semantic link between political intrigue and amorous infidelity. But "Labour to'admit you" implies that "three person'd God" is there at the gates, besieging the "usurpt towne" in the person of a monarch reclaiming his territory.

—William Kerrigan, "The Fearful Accommodations of John Donne," *English Literary Renaissance* 4, no. 3 (Autumn 1974): pp. 337–38, 340, 351.

Works by
John Donne

Biathanatos. 1608.

Pseudo-Martyr. 1610.

The Courtier's Library. 1611.

Ignatius His Conclave. 1611

The First and Second Anniversaries. 1612.

Essays in Divinity. c. 1615

Devotions Upon Emergent Occasions. 1624.

Death's Duel. c. 1628.

Songs and Sonnets. 1633.

Holy Sonnets. 1635.

Works about
John Donne

Andreasen, N.J.C. *John Donne: Conservative Revolutionary*. Princeton: Princeton University Press, 1967.

Bald R.C. *John Donne: A Life*. Oxford: Clarendon Press, 1970.

Carey, John. *John Donne: Life, Mind and Art*. London, Faber and Faber, 1990.

Coffin, Charles M. *John Donne and The New Philosophy*. New York: Columbia University Press, 1937.

Colie, Rosalie. *Paradoxia Epdiemica: The Renaissance Tradition of Paradox*. Princeton: Princeton University Press, 1966.

Davis, Herbert, and Helen Gardner, eds. *Elizabethan and Jacobean Studies Presented to Frank Percy Williams*. Oxford: Oxford University Press, 1959.

Ferry, Anne. *The 'Inward' Language: Sonnets of Wyatt, Sidney, Shakespeare, Donne*. Chicago: University of Chicago Press, 1983.

Fish, Stanley E. *Self-Consuming Artifacts: The Experience of Seventeenth-Century Literature*. Berkeley/ Los Angeles: University of California Press, 1972.

Flynn, Dennis. *Donne and the Ancient Catholic Nobility*. Bloomington and Indianapolis: Indiana University Press, 1995.

Goldberg, Jonathan. *James I and the Politics of Literature: Jonson, Shakespeare, Donne and Their Contemporaries*. Baltimore: Johns Hopkins University Press, 1983.

Guss, Donald L. *John Donne, Petrarchist: Italianate Conceits and Love Theory in the* Songs and Sonnets. Detroit: Wayne State University Press, 1966.

Hunt, Clay. *Donne's Poetry: Essays in Literary Analysis*. New Haven: Yale University Press, 1954.

Legouis, Pierre. *Donne the Craftsman: An Essay upon the Structure of the* Songs and Sonnets. New York: Russel and Russel, 1962.

Leishman, J.B. *The Monarch of Wit*. London: Hutchinson, 1962.

Lewalski, Barbara K. *Protestant Poetics and the Seventeenth-Century Religious Lyric*. Princeton: Princeton University Press, 1979.

Lewis, C. S. *Seventeenth Century Studies Presented to Sir Herbert Grierson*. Oxford: Oxford University Press, 1938.

Low, Anthony. *Love's Architecture: Devotional Modes in Seventeenth-Century English Poetry*. New York: New York University Press, 1978.

Marotti, Arthur F. *John Donne, Coterie Poet*. Madison: University of Wisconsin Press, 1986.

Martz, Louis L. *From Renaissance to Baroque: Essays on Literature and Art.* Columbia: University of Missouri Press, 1962.

Miner, Earl. *The Metaphysical Mode from Donne to Cowley.* Princeton: Princeton University Press, 1969.

Mueller, William R. *John Donne: Preacher.* Princeton: Princeton University Press, 1962.

Nicholson, Marjorie Hope. *The Breaking of the Circle: Studies in the Effect of the "New Science" upon Seventeenth-Century Poetry.* New York: Columbia University Press, 1960.

Novaar, David. *The Disinterred Muse: Donne's Texts and Contexts.* Ithaca: Cornell University Press, 1958.

Sanders, Wilbur. *John Donne's Poetry.* Cambridge: Cambridge University Press, 1971.

Sherwood, Terry G. *Fulfilling the Circle: A Study of John Donne's Thought.* Toronto: University of Toronto Press, 1984.

Shuger, Debora Kuller. *Habits of Thought in the English Renaissance: Religion, Politics, and the Dominant Culture.* Berkeley/Los Angeles: University of California Press, 1990.

Simpson, Evelyn M. *A Study of the Prose Works of John Donne,* 2nd edition, Oxford: Clarendon Press, 1948.

Spencer, Theodore, ed. *A Garland for John Donne, 1631–1931.* Cambridge: Harvard University Press, 1931.

Stanwood, P.G., and Heather Ross Asals, ed. *John Donne and the Theology of Language.* Columbia: University of Missouri Press, 1986.

Stein, Arnold. *John Donne's Lyrics: The Eloquence of Action.* Minneapolis: University of Minnesota Press, 1962.

Summers, Claude J. and Ted-Larry Pebworth, eds., *The Eagle and the Dove: Reassessing John Donne.* Columbia: University of Missouri Press, 1986.

Webber, Joan. *Contrary Music: The Prose Style of John Donne.* Madison: University of Wisconsin Press, 1963.

Williamson, George. *The Donne Tradition: A Study in English Poetry from Donne to the Death of Cowley.* New York: Noonday Press, 1930.

Woodbridge, Linda. *Woman and the English Renaissance: Literature and the Nature of Womankind, 1540–1620.* Urbana: University of Illinois Press, 1984.

Index of
Themes and Ideas